MW00526989

To:

_____

From:

_____

Date:

_____

Message:

_____

_____

_____

_____

_____

_____

The Devotional for Busy People

Simple and Powerful Truth
to Help Jump Start Your Day

GBENGA ASEDEKO

Gbenga Asedeko
El Paso. Texas

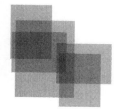

THE DEVOTIONAL FOR BUSY PEOPLE: SIMPLE AND POWERFUL TRUTH TO HELP JUMP START YOUR DAY

Copyright © 2014 by Gbenga Asedeko
Published by Gbenga Asedeko
El Paso, Texas

www.GbengaAsedeko.com

ISBN-13: 978-0692346372
ISBN-10: 0692346376

Cover design by Creative Gong, LLC
Printed in the United States of America

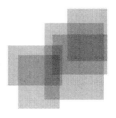

The Devotional
for Busy People

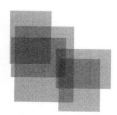

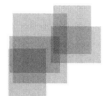

Introduction

Life is busy and as a result we get caught up in the demands of the urgent, the pressure of dead lines, and the pull on our attention from multiple directions. It seems unrelenting from the moment we start our day until we finally collapse at its end. We get so overwhelmed by the frenzy of activity that we tend to forget one of the most important foundations for our lives... our spirituality. The Devotional For Busy People will help you, in less than a minute, develop and keep your spiritual foundation.

It has been said that how you start your day determines how you will end your day. Author and motivational speaker Gbenga Asedeko adds one more element to that saying... "How you start your day impacts your entire day and lasts all the way to its end." His own experience has confirmed this great truth so much so that he began to journal a devotional thought for each day of the year. It was so dynamic and powerful in his own life that he published his writings for you to discover and benefit from them in The Devotional For Busy People.

Gbenga has stated, "I was controlled by fear, depression, addiction, frustration, stress and many other limitations. I overcame, and I'm still overcoming, by doing simple things daily. One of those simple things is starting each and every day with a devotional thought and prayer. The Devotional For Busy People was written from painful and successful experiences of my life as well as from the lives of many others. It has encouraged many during difficult times in their personal and professional lives."

The Devotional for Busy People will not only help you to jumpstart your day, it will help you develop your personal relationship with God and become passionately interested in spiritual matters. In less than a minute you will connect to the Source of life, peace, joy, health, wisdom, protection, freedom, victory, and prosperity. Consistently reading from The Devotional for Busy People will help bring you a needed breakthrough, find victory in the battle of life, and witness personal transformation.

In less than a minute each day you can have 24 hours of positive benefit. Where else can you invest less than one tenth of one percent to reap so much in the end.

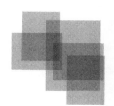

Day 1
Be Bold!

"Let us therefore come boldly unto the throne of grace, that we may obtain mercy, and find grace to help in time of need."

Hebrews 4:16

Go boldly to God concerning the big and the small things you desire in your life. He will give you mercy and grace (unmerited and undeserved favor) to help in time of need. Don't allow any situation to contain you; break out and break loose! Let hope rise up on the inside of you. ARISE and go. Be bold; don't be timid! Amen.

*Lord, give me the grace to come boldly unto Your throne of grace daily. I receive your mercy and grace for every area of my life in Jesus' name.
Amen.*

_____
_____
_____
_____

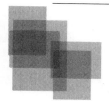

Simple and Powerful Truth to help Jump Start Your Day

Day 2
Be Confident!

"Being confident of this very thing, that he which hath begun a good work in you will perform it until the day of Jesus Christ."

Philippians 1:6

God does not start something and complete it halfway. Be confident that Lord will complete the good work He has begun in your health, businesses, finances and relationships. That situation might seem difficult, but it's temporary. God will finish what He started in your life. Victory is yours! Amen.

Lord, give me the grace to trust You to finish the good work You have begun in me. I receive Your peace into my life in Jesus' name.
Amen.

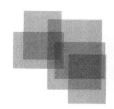

Day 3
Joy is Coming!

"For his anger endures but a moment; in his favor is life: weeping may endure for a night, but joy comes in the morning."

Psalms 30:5

I don't know what is confronting you and what you are going through, but God promises that your weeping (crying, trials, pain, lacks, health problem, and anything that is holding you back) is coming to an end. Joy is coming! Get ready for your victory dance. Amen.

Lord, give me the grace to focus on the Joy that is coming, my victory and breakthroughs and not the situation confronting me, in Jesus' name.
Amen.

_____

_____

_____

_____

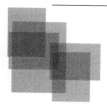

Simple and Powerful Truth to help Jump Start Your Day

Day 4
You are Favored!

*"And the angel said unto her,
'Fear not, Mary: for thou hast
found favor with God.'"*

Luke 1:30

Fear not, for you have found favor with God. Don't fear weakness, financial difficulty, limitations in your life, those that come against you, because you have found profound favor with God. The favor of God will do the impossible in your life. You are favored! Amen.

*Lord, I thank You for Your favor in my life. Give me
the grace to be favor minded in Jesus' name.
Amen*

_____

_____

_____

_____

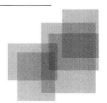

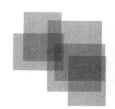

Day 5
Sooner or Later!

"Ask, and it will be given to you;
seek, and you will find; knock,
and it will be opened to you.
For everyone who asks receives,
and he who seeks finds, and to him
who knocks it will be opened."

Matthew 7:7-8

Keep on asking, keep on seeking, keep on knocking. Sooner or later God will open the doors of blessings and opportunities at the right time, doors no man can close for you. Our God is a faithful God. Keep trusting in Him and before you know it, things you prayed about will come to pass! Amen.

Lord, give me the grace to not give up in the midst of
that difficult situation. Help me to keep on believing,
doing my best and to keep on trusting in You,
in Jesus' name.
Amen.

_____

_____

_____

_____

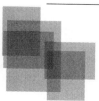

Simple and Powerful Truth to help Jump Start Your Day

Day 6
Not in Vain!

"Therefore, my dear brothers and sisters, stand firm. Let nothing move you. Always give yourselves fully to the work of the Lord, because you know that your labor in the Lord is not in vain."

I Corinthians 15:58

My friend, you have been praying, giving and doing your best to live your life to honor God. You have been laboring with your life, family, finances, health, job, business and relationships. Know today that your labor is not vain. His goodness will soon overflow your life. Get ready! Amen.

*Lord, give me the grace to continue to serve You
and to do what's right in the face of challenges
of life in Jesus' name.
Amen.*

_____

_____

_____

_____

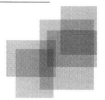

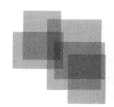

Day 7
Give Thanks!

"O give thanks to the Lord,
for He is good; for His mercy and
loving-kindness endure forever."

Psalms 136:1 (AMP)

The Lord wants to be good to you today. Don't only give thanks for what you desire for your life; also give thanks to the Lord for His goodness. God is good and He wants to be good to you. Always remember this in the face of a difficult situation.

Lord, I thank You, for You are good and have been
good to me. Give me the grace to always remember
Your goodness in my life in Jesus' name.
Amen.

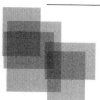

Simple and Powerful Truth to help Jump Start Your Day

Day 8
It's Possible!

"But Jesus looked at them and said, "With men it is impossible, but not with God; for with God all things are possible."

Mark 10:27

What's transpiring in your life right now might seem impossible, but with God nothing is impossible. Keep doing your best and keep trusting in God. Say this out loud: "Lord, I still believe." It's too late to give up. Let hope rise up on the inside of you. It's possible with our God my friend!

Lord, I thank You for performing the impossible in my life. Thank you for giving me the grace to trust in You in Jesus' name.
Amen.

_____

_____

_____

_____

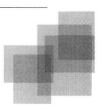

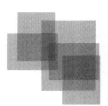

Day 9
If You Can Believe...

*"Jesus said to him,
if you can believe, all things are
possible to him who believes."*

Mark 9:23

Don't allow any situation to stop you from believing. If you can continue to believe, all things are possible. Believe that God is giving you wisdom to create wealth, restoring what has been stolen in your life, fighting your battles for you, giving you favor and making a way for you. All we need to do is believe all things are possible! Amen.

*Lord, give me the grace to continue to believe in You
in all circumstances of life in Jesus' name.
Amen.*

_____

_____

_____

_____

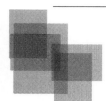

14

Day 10
His Thoughts Are Good

*"I know the thoughts that I
think toward you, says the Lord,
thoughts of peace and not of evil,
to give you a future and a hope."*

Jeremiah 29:11

In God you have a future and hope. God thinks very highly of you at all times in spite of your mistakes, weaknesses and shortcomings. He wants to be good to you, so don't think less of yourself. Let hope rise up on the inside of you; your best is yet to come. He is thinking of you. Amen.

*Lord, I thank You for thinking good thoughts towards
me and thank You that You are causing me to fulfill
Your destiny for my life in Jesus' name.
Amen.*

_____

_____

_____

_____

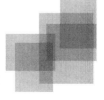

Day 11
He Makes Ways!

*"Thus says the Lord, Who makes
a way through the sea and a path
through the mighty waters..."*

Isaiah 43:16

Our God makes a way for us. Though we confront difficult situations,
He makes a way. My friend, just trust in Him; He will make a way where
you think there is no way. God will do for you what you can't do in your
own strength and wisdom. He will make a way for you. Amen.

*Lord, I thank You for making a way for me and for
Your favor in my life in Jesus' name.
Amen.*

_____

_____

_____

_____

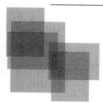

Simple and Powerful Truth to help Jump Start Your Day

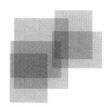

Day 12
More and More

"But I will hope continually,
and will praise You yet more and
more."

Psalms 71:14

You have heard the saying, "When the going gets tough, the tough get going." There's no need to worry if that situation is taking a long time or about how far you still need to go. Continue to hope in God and praise Him more and more in the midst of that difficulty. When you entrust God in your life, you will know the peace of God. He will saturate your mind with wisdom and lead you in the path of victory. Amen.

Lord, give me the grace to hope in You and praise
You continually. I thank You for more and more of
Your blessings and favor in my life in Jesus' name.
Amen.

Day 13
Power, Love and Sound Mind

*"For God hath not given us the
spirit of fear; but of power, and of
love, and of a sound mind."*

2 Timothy 1:7

What are you afraid of? Are you afraid about your life, health, family, finances, business or a particular relationship? Fear is not of God, but of the enemy. The enemy uses fear to prevent us from trusting in God. When fear tries to overtake you, reject it and declare the spirit of power, love and sound mind over your life. Amen.

Lord, I thank You for giving me victory over fear.
I receive Your Spirit of power, love and sound mind
in Jesus' name.
Amen.

_____

_____

_____

_____

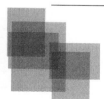

Simple and Powerful Truth to help Jump Start Your Day

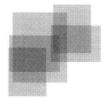

Day 14
Promises Kept!

"For all the promises of God in Him are Yes, and in Him Amen, to the glory of God through us."

2 Corinthians 1:20

All the promises from God concerning every area of your life have been kept through the death of His Son our Savior Jesus Christ. When you are confronted with difficult situations, remember God's promise. Remember Christ has already paid the price for that promise. All you need to do is to believe and receive His promise into your life. Amen.

Lord, I thank You, for You are a promise keeper.
Give me the grace to believe and receive Your
promises into my life in Jesus' name.
Amen.

_____

_____

_____

_____

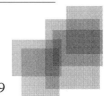

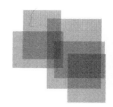

Day 15
Turn Around!

"You intended to harm me, but God intended it for good to accomplish what is now being done, the saving of many lives"

Genesis 50:20 (NIV)

Joseph's brothers hated him, tried to kill him and sold him to slavery. Their intentions were to harm and destroy his life. But God turned their intended harm around to elevate Joseph. Turnaround is coming into your life, your finances, your health, your marriage and into your relationships. God will turn around that difficult situation and use it to elevate you. Be turnaround-minded. Amen.

Lord,
I thank You for turning around things in my favor.
Give me the grace to be favor and
turnaround-minded in Jesus' name.
Amen.

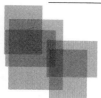

Simple and Powerful Truth to help Jump Start Your Day

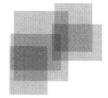

Day 16
All is Well!

*"Say to the righteous that it shall
be well with them..."*

Isaiah 3:10

My friend, no matter what is going on in your life, I say to you, "All is well." God is faithful and He will not leave you in that situation. He will turn it around for your good. In the midst of that difficult situation, say, "All is well." When you say, "All is well," you are trusting that God will make a way, that He will open new doors, that He will heal, deliver you and give you strength and the wisdom you need. All is well with you. Amen.

*Lord, give me the grace to have the mindset of
believing and declaring that it's well at all times
in Jesus' name.
Amen.*

_____

_____

_____

_____

Day 17
He'll Never Fail You!

*"...I will not in any way fail you
nor give you up nor leave you
without support... "*

Hebrews 13:5 (AMP)

You might be down, dealing with a difficult situation or a relationship. You might feel you have tried all that you could do, but nothing seems to be working as desired. Trust in God. He has promised to not fail you in any way or leave you without support. Our God will never fail you! Get back up. Amen.

*Lord, give me the grace to believe at all times that
You will never fail me. I thank You for Your never
failing love in Jesus' name.
Amen.*

Day 18
The Name of Jesus

"Therefore God also has highly exalted Him and given Him the name which is above every name, that at the name of Jesus every knee should bow, of those in heaven, and of those on earth, and of those under the earth."

Philippians 2:9-10

The name of Jesus is greater than anything confronting you. Whatever is confronting you has a name (sickness, lack, depression, marriage trouble, troubled child, business crisis, loss of a job, relationship problem, etc.), and that name must bow to the name of Jesus. Use the name of Jesus for that situation confronting you. That situation will bow to His name. Amen.

Lord, I thank you for your freedom, healing, deliverance, favor and wisdom over my life and over that situation confronting me in the name of Jesus. Amen

_____

_____

_____

_____

Day 19
His Faithfulness

"If we are unfaithful,
He remains faithful,
for He cannot deny who He is."

2 Timothy 2:13

God is faithful in spite of your unfaithfulness and He still wants to be good to you. Don't allow your shortcomings, regrets or condemnation to stop you from believing. The faithfulness and the goodness of God is greater than your past, present and future shortcomings. God is not mad at you; He wants to amaze you with His goodness. Amen.

Lord, I thank You that You are faithful to me even
when I'm unfaithful to You. Give me the grace to be
faithful to You in Jesus' name.
Amen.

_____

_____

_____

_____

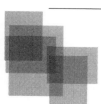

Day 20
Unconditional Love

*"But God demonstrates His own
love toward us, in that while we
were still sinners, Christ died for
us."*

Romans 5:8

You didn't do anything to earn the love of God and you can't do
anything to lose His love. He loves you unconditionally in spite of your
shortcomings. Always remember His unconditional love for you when
you feel lonely, when you feel like everything is coming against you and
when things seem impossible. Our loving Aba Father will never leave you
without help. Amen.

*Lord, I thank You for Your unconditional love.
Give me the grace to fully enjoy Your love
and grace to allow Your love to flow through
me to others in Jesus' name.
Amen.*

Day 21
The Very Present Help

"God is our refuge and strength,
a very present help in trouble."

Psalms 46:1

Maybe you're in trouble or been confronted with a difficult situation. Don't give up; God is able, willing and ready to help. Keep doing your best and keep on trusting in Him. He is your refuge, strength and helper. God is the very present help in times of trouble. My friend, help is on the way!

Lord, I thank You for You are my present help in
times of trouble. Give me the grace to keep on
trusting in You in Jesus name.
Amen.

_____

_____

_____

_____

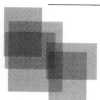

26

Day 22
Don't Give Up Hope!

*"Return to the stronghold (of
security and prosperity), you
prisoners of hope; even today do
I declare that I will restore double
your former prosperity to you."*

Zechariah 9:12

Don't go by what you see; go by what you believe. What you see might
not make sense or add up, but God will keep His promises of restoration,
abundance and healing in your life. Keep hoping in God. He promised to
give you double of His goodness, double of His favor, double of everything
that pertains to life and godliness. Don't give up hope. Amen.

*Lord, give me the grace to become a prisoner of
Hope in Jesus' name.
Amen.*

_____

_____

_____

_____

Day 23
Taste and See!

"Oh taste and see that the Lord is good; blessed is the man who trusts in Him."

Psalm 34:8

My friend look around you and look in your life, you will see the goodness of God all over. When you thank God for His goodness instead of focusing on what you don't have, you will experience (taste and see) more of the goodness of God in every area of your life. Don't look at how difficult things are – look at how good God is. You're blessed. Amen.

Lord, give me the grace to focus on Your goodness in my life. I declare that I will taste and see Your goodness in every area of my life in Jesus' name.
Amen.

_____

_____

_____

_____

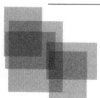

28

Day 24
Grace

*"But He said to me, my grace (My favor
and loving-kindness and mercy) is enough
for you (sufficient against any danger and
enables you to bear the trouble manfully);
for My strength and power are made
perfect (fulfilled and completed) and show
themselves most effective in your weakness."*

2 Corinthians 12:9

No matter what you are going through, the grace of the Almighty God is
more than enough for you to overcome. You are not alone; His grace is
enough for you. He will make a way for you where there seems to be no
way. He will restore, and perfect everything that concerns you. Rest on His
grace! Amen.

*Lord, give me the grace to fully rely on Your grace
for every area of my life in Jesus' name.
Amen.*

_____

_____

_____

_____

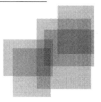

Day 25
God Knows!

*"I declare the end from the
beginning, and from long ago what
is not yet done, saying: My plan will
take place, and I will do all My will."*

Isaiah 46:10

God is not surprised about what is going on in your life. He knows what
He's doing. He knows everything about that situation and He is working
things out in your favor. Don't stop believing and don't give up your hope
in Him. At the time you least expect He will turn things around in your
favor. He knows what He's doing. Amen.

Lord,
I thank You for working all things out in my favor.
I trust in You in Jesus' name.
Amen.

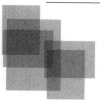

30

Day 26
Lord, I Believe!

"Immediately the father of the
child cried out and said with
tears, "Lord, I believe; help my
unbelief!"

Mark 9:24

Maybe you feel overwhelmed by a situation and you have little or no strength, like the father in the verse above, to continue to believe. When you're weak, God becomes strong for you. I pray that God will help you with your unbelief. Say out loud, "Lord, I believe."

Lord, help my unbelief in Jesus' name.
Amen.

_____

_____

_____

_____

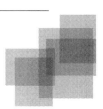

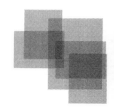

Day 27
I Still Believe!

"Now faith is the substance of things hoped for, the evidence of things no seen"

Hebrews 11:1

You have heard the saying, "I will believe it when I see it." If you don't see it, will you still believe it? Believe first! Believe the promises of God about your health, abundance, favor, wisdom, protection, etc. When you keep on believing and declaring His promises over your life, you will begin to see them manifest in your life. I still believe in the faithfulness of God. Amen.

*Lord, give me the grace to consistently believe in
You and Your promises for my life in Jesus' name.
Amen.*

_____

_____

_____

_____

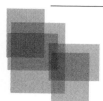

Simple and Powerful Truth to help Jump Start Your Day

Day 28
God Day is Good!

*"For the Lord is good and
His love endures forever; His
faithfulness continues through all
generations."*

Psalms 100:5

God is good not only in good times, but in bad times as well. He is good
at all times. God wants to be good to you in the midst of that difficult
situation. Believe and receive His goodness into your life, not only in good
times, but also in moments of great difficulties. Say it out loud:
"Lord, I receive Your goodness into my life. Amen."

*Lord, give me the grace to receive Your goodness
for every area of my life in Jesus' name.
Amen.*

Day 29
Stand In Awe of Him!

"Let all the earth fear the Lord:
let all the inhabitants of the world
stand in awe of him."

Psalm 33:8

Who and what you respect and honor will respect and honor you. Who and what you pay attention to will affect the course of your day. I encourage you today to stand in awe (wonder, admiration, respect, surprise, wonderment and astonishment) of God. Our God is an awesome God. Stand in awe of Him by worshiping and giving Him thanks.
I love You, Lord. Amen.

Lord, I stand in awe of You. Cause me to be
overwhelmed by Your awesomeness in every facets
of my life in Jesus' name.
Amen.

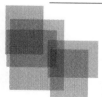

34

Day 30
Rejoice!

*"Rejoice in the Lord always.
Again I will say, rejoice"*

Philippians 4:4

Are you in a rejoicing mood or in a worry mood? Worrying is not going to change anything; in fact, it will make things worse. Always rejoice in the Lord, not in your problems. You are not rejoicing for the difficult times you are going through but for the things God has provided for you. The Lord is your provider, healer, deliverer and Savior. He keeps His promises for every area of your life. Again, I say to rejoice, because help is on the way. Amen.

*Lord, give me the grace to always rejoice in You
in Jesus' name.
Amen.*

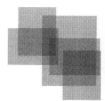

Day 31
Rich and Satisfying Life

"The thief's purpose is to steal and kill and destroy. My purpose is to give them a rich and satisfying life."

John 10:10

What the enemy has stolen, God will restore back to you. What the enemy has killed, God will breath life into. And what he has destroyed, God will restore back to you in multiple folds. It is not over, my friend. In the midst of that situation envision an abundant, rich and satisfying life. Amen.

Lord, I thank You for giving me a rich and satisfying life. Give me the grace to enjoy this life to the fullest in Jesus' name.
Amen.

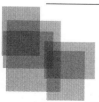

Simple and Powerful Truth to help Jump Start Your Day

Day 32
Victory is Yours!

"But thanks be to God! He gives us the victory through our Lord Jesus Christ."

1 Corinthians 15:57

No matter what is confronting you, God already gave you the victory through our Lord Jesus Christ. Instead of worrying about that situation, thank God for your victory. God loves you, believes in you and wants the best for you in spite of how difficult that situation is and in spite of your shortcomings. Do not ever give up. Victory is yours! Amen.

I declare new mercies, favor, wisdom, strength and new ideas into your life. Victory is yours in Jesus' name.
Amen.

_____

_____

_____

_____

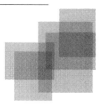

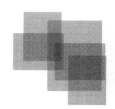

Day 33
The Refresher

"He refreshes my soul.
He guides me along the right paths
for His name's sake."

Psalms 23:3

Allow God to refresh your soul. God wants to revive, invigorate, rejuvenate, energize, restore, recharge and revitalize every area of your life. No matter how down you are or how far you think you've gone, God wants to refresh your soul. He is your refresher. Get back up and get your praise on. Put on good Christian music and focus on His goodness. Amen.

I declare that God will lead you in the right path
to victory and breakthrough and that your soul is
refreshed by His goodness in Jesus' name.
Amen.

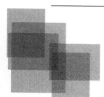

Day 34
Do Not Fear!

"The Lord is on my side;
I will not fear.
What can man do to me?"

Psalms 118:6

Do not fear that financial difficulty, troubled child, spouse, boss, health problem or anything confronting you because the Lord is on your side. The main purpose of fear to stop you from enjoying the promises of God and the reality of the fact that God is with you. Do not allow fear to dominate your life; instead feed your mind daily with the promises of God.

Lord, I thank You for Your victory over the spirit of
fear and I thank You for choosing to be on my side.
I declare that victory is mine in Jesus' name.
Amen.

Day 35
More Than Enough Grace

*"But He said to me, "My grace is
sufficient for you, for my power is
made perfect in weakness...""*

2 Corinthians 12:9

Say this out loud: "Father God, I submit this situation to You. I trust in You
and I receive Your grace to sustain me. Thank you for the wisdom to make
wise decisions and to cause me to overcome." My friend, the grace of God
is more than enough for anything confronting you. Trust in Him to do for
you what you can't do in your own power and in your own strength.

*Lord, I receive Your more than enough grace for
every area of my life in Jesus' name.
Amen.*

_____

_____

_____

_____

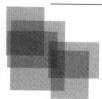

Simple and Powerful Truth to help Jump Start Your Day

Day 36
Nothing Impossible!

*"For nothing is
impossible with God."*

Luke 1:37

Nothing is impossible with our God, and that includes the situation
confronting you. My friend, here is the good news: God is not surprised
about what's confronting you. He already won the victory for you.
Believe and trust in Him. Let hope rise up on the inside of you.
With Him, nothing is ever impossible!

*Lord, I thank You for doing the impossible in my
finances, health, children, marriage, business, my
job and in every area of my life in Jesus' name.
Amen.*

_____

_____

_____

_____

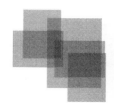

Day 37
Blessings

*"May the Lord bless you
and protect you."*

Numbers 6:24

Expect the blessings and the protection of God in every area of your life today.

God wants to overwhelm you with His goodness in every of your life. I declare the blessings and protection of God over your life, business, job, finance, health and relationships in Jesus' name. Believe it and receive it into your life. Amen.

*Lord, I receive Your blessings into my life
in Jesus' name.
Amen.*

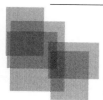

42

Day 38
The Present Help

*"God is our refuge and strength,
an ever-present help in times
of trouble."*

Psalms 46:1

It's okay to cry in the midst of difficult situations. Cry, but also cry out to God who is willing, ready and able to help. He is your ever-present help in times of trouble.

Ask God for help today, and He will gladly help you and give you peace and restoration concerning that situation. He is your present help. Amen.

*Lord, give me the grace to rely on You at all times
in Jesus' name.
Amen.*

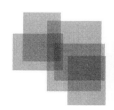

Day 39
The Nearby God

*"The Lord is near to all who
call on Him..."*

Psalms 145:18

God is not far away from you. As a matter of fact, He lives inside of you. Call on Him concerning your situation. He will answer with freedom, wisdom, favor, projection, restoration, abundance, grace and anything that you need. The nearby God will always answer when you call upon His name. Victory is yours in Jesus' name. Amen.

*Lord, I thank you for being on my side and for living
in me. Give me the grace to fully comprehend how
close You are to me in Jesus' name.
Amen.*

_____

_____

_____

_____

Simple and Powerful Truth to help Jump Start Your Day

Day 40
Victory Assured

"But thanks be to God,
which gives us the victory through
our Lord Jesus Christ."

1 Corinthians 15:57

God is fighting your battles for you; as a matter of fact, He already won the battle for you. Your victory is assured, so let hope rise up on the inside of you. The enemy has been defeated concerning the situation confronting you. Be victory-minded today.

Lord, I thank You for fighting my battles for me
and for giving me victory in Jesus' name.
Amen.

Day 41
Exceeding Abundantly

"Now unto Him that is able to do exceeding abundantly above all that we ask or think..."

Ephesians 3:20

God will amaze you with His goodness and He will do so in exceeding abundance above all that you ask or think. He will open doors no man can close; He will break chains of addictions that have been holding you for years. He will restore your marriage and relationships that matter to you. You will experience the exceeding abundance of God's goodness in your life. Believe and receive it. Amen.

Lord, I receive Your exceedingly abundant bountiful
blessings in every area of my life in Jesus' name.
Amen.

_____

_____

_____

_____

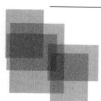

Simple and Powerful Truth to help Jump Start Your Day

Day 42
The Light of Life

"When Jesus spoke again to the people, He said, "I am the light of the world. Whoever follows me will never walk in darkness, but will have the light of life."

John 8:12

Jesus is the light of your life and I pray that His glorious light will shine into every situation confronting you. Any darkness in any area of your life will disappear through the glorious light of our Lord Jesus Christ. God will give you the wisdom to make wise decisions. Amen.

Lord, shine Your glorious light in my life and in
every situation confronting me in Jesus' name.
Amen.

_____

_____

_____

_____

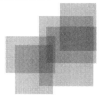

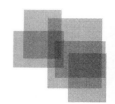

Day 43
I Can!

*"I can do all things through Christ
who gives me strength."*

Philippians 4:13

When your strength fails, the strength of God kicks in. You have the strength to overcome, to do anything you need to do today, because the strength, the infusion of power into your life through our Lord and Savior Jesus Christ. Do not focus on your ability; instead focus on His strength today. Amen.

*Lord, give me the grace to completely rely on Your
strength at all times in Jesus' name.
Amen.*

_____

_____

_____

_____

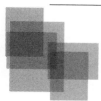

Simple and Powerful Truth to help Jump Start Your Day

Day 44
Engraved

"See, I have engraved you on the palms of my hands; your walls are ever before me."

Isaiah 49:16

The Lord has engraved you on the palms of His hands. That means no weapon formed against you shall prosper. The enemy might attack things and people might be coming against you, but they cannot break you. Your life has been engraved through the blood of our Lord and Savoir Jesus Christ. Amen.

Lord, I thank You for engraving me in the palms of Your hands. I declare that you will experience the fullness of God's blessings in every areas of your life in Jesus' name.
Amen.

_____

_____

_____

_____

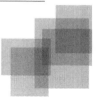

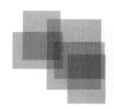

45
Arise and Shine!

"Arise, shine, for your light has come, and the glory of the Lord is rises upon you."

Isaiah 60:1

The glory of the Lord is over every area of your life. It's all well with you in Jesus' name. My friend, this is your time to shine. Your struggles are coming to an end. Arise and shine because the victory has been won for you in Jesus' name. Amen.

> *Lord, give me the grace to arise and shine into the*
> *destiny You have for me and into the blessings You*
> *have in store for me in Jesus' name.*
> *Amen.*

_____

_____

_____

_____

Simple and Powerful Truth to help Jump Start Your Day

46
Good Things

"For the Lord God is a sun and shield; The Lord will give grace and glory; No good thing will He withhold from those who walk uprightly."

Psalms 84:11

We serve a good God who wants to be good to you. What good things do you desire for different areas of your life? God will not withhold them from you. Believe in Him for good things in your health, finances, business, and relationships.

I declare that you will experience super abounding goodness of God in every area of your life in Jesus' name. Amen.

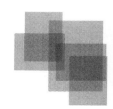

Day 47
The Same Every Day

*"Jesus Christ the same yesterday,
and today, and forever."*

Hebrews 13:8

Friends and family might ignore or betray you, but not Jesus. He is the same every day no matter what you've done or will do. He is your friend and Savior. He will be there with you in your highest and at your lowest moments. His love for you is not conditional on anything you have done or will ever do. Know that God is with you. He is the same every day! Amen.

*Lord, I thank You that Your love for me never
changes. Give me the grace to live my life to honor
you daily in Jesus's name.
Amen.*

_____

_____

_____

_____

Simple and Powerful Truth to help Jump Start Your Day

Day 48
You Are Covered!

*"But You, O Lord, are a shield for
me, My glory and the One who
lifts up my head."*

Psalms 3:3

The Lord is your shield of favor, wisdom and protection. He will shield you from evil and destruction. You might be going through a valley; the Lord will shield you to the mountaintop. He is your glory and He will cause your mouth to be filled with praise. Don't dwell on that situation with your head hanging down; the Lord is the lifter of your head. You are covered, my friend. Amen.

*Lord, I thank You for shielding me with Your favor,
wisdom and protection. I thank You, for You are
my glory and the lifter of my head. I walk in Your
victory today in Jesus' name.
Amen.*

_____

_____

_____

_____

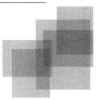

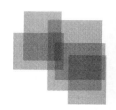

Day 49
Our God is Greater!

*"You are of God, little children,
and have overcome them, because
He who is in you is greater than he
who is in the world."*

1 John 4:4

Our God is greater, stronger and much more powerful than anything confronting you. Our God is for you. He is on your side and He promised to never leave you or forsake you. You are not going under – you are going over the top. Go on and live your life today and every day with great expectation. Our God is greater than anything confronting you.

*Lord, I thank You that You are greater that any
situation confronting me. Give me the grace to live
in the greatness of your power in Jesus' name.
Amen.*

_____

_____

_____

_____

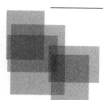

Simple and Powerful Truth to help Jump Start Your Day

Day 50
You're an Overcomer!

"For whatever is born of God
overcomes the world. And this is
the victory that has overcome
the world — our faith."

1 John 5:4

You are an overcomer in spite of what is going on in your life, in spite of what you don't have, in spite of your shortcomings, in spite of what people think or say about you and in spite of who or what is coming against you. You have the victory in the name of Jesus.

I declare that you will overcome that situation.
You are victorious in Jesus' name.
Amen.

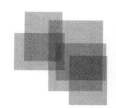

Day 51
Suddenly

"For the Lord your God is He
who goes with you, to fight for you
against your enemies, to save you."

Deuteronomy 20:4

You have been praying, trusting, and hoping for an answer to your prayers. When you least expect, when you feel like giving up, God will show up suddenly and will amaze you with His goodness. You will suddenly have your breakthrough and freedom. You will become debt-free, healed, have sudden divine opportunities and divine connections. Instead of barely getting by, you will have more than enough. Expect the sudden goodness of God today. Amen.

Lord, I thank You for fighting my battles for me and
for you sudden goodness in my life in Jesus' name.
Amen.

_____

_____

_____

_____

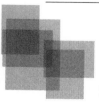

Simple and Powerful Truth to help Jump Start Your Day

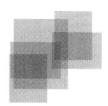

Day 52
Eventually

"And let us not grow weary while doing good, for in due season we shall reap if we do not lose heart."

Galatians 6:9

In the midst of that difficult situation, keep on giving, believing, praying, loving and praising. Eventually, if you don't give up and lose heart you will reap the abundance of God's blessings in your life. You will experience a breakthrough and experience the divine favor of God. Eventually, God will turn around that situation in your favor! Amen.

Lord, give me the grace to not grow weary
in doing good in Jesus' name.
Amen.

_____

_____

_____

_____

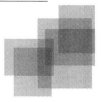

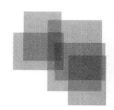

Day 53
He Is Strong for You!

"And He said to me, "My grace is sufficient for you, for My strength is made perfect in weakness."

2 Corinthians 12:9

When you are weak, God's will steps in and becomes strong for you. When you have no strength to keep believing, God will step in and help your unbelief. When you are faithless, the faith of God will kick in and carry you through. My friend, God is always strong for you. Remember this when the going gets tough. You are not alone. He is with you, He is alongside you and He is strong for you. Amen.

Lord, I thank You that Your grace is sufficient for me.
I rely on Your grace for every area of my life
in Jesus' name.
Amen.

_____

_____

_____

_____

Day 54
Memories

"As far as the east is from the west, So far has He removed our transgressions from us."

Psalms 103:12

God is not keeping a record of your wrongdoings and your mistakes. He does not judge or criticize you; before you sinned He had already forgiven you. Have a great opinion of yourself. Don't judge yourself and don't allow the criticism of others to control your life. The memories of your wrongdoings are nonexistent with our God. Keep doing your best to live your life to honor God. Move your life forward free of bad memories. Amen.

Lord, give me the grace to live my life to honor You, and when I fall give me the grace to receive Your forgiveness and strength to do better in Jesus' name. Amen.

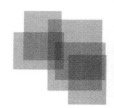

Day 55
He Remembers!

"Can a woman forget her nursing child,
And not have compassion on the son of
her womb? Surely they may forget, Yet I
will not forget you. See, I have inscribed
you on the palms of My hands;
Your walls are continually before Me."

Isaiah 49:15-16

God will open the book of remembrance concerning you. He sees your struggles, your weakness. He knows about your pain, your giving, your praying and your believing. He has not forgotten about you. Let hope rise up on the inside of you. He remembers and He promises to bless you abundantly! Amen.

Lord, I thank You for opening the book of
remembrance concerning every area of my life in
Jesus' name.
Amen.

_____

_____

_____

_____

60

Day 56
He Is Your Friend!

*"No longer do I call you servants,
for a servant does not know what
his master is doing; but I have
called you friends..."*

John 15:15

You're a friend of God, and He calls you friend. Friends and family might forsake you, talk about you, break a promise and betray you. Jesus will not; He is your friend. He will always be there when you need Him. He loves you with all your weaknesses and He believes in you. When you're lonely or frustrated or need wisdom or someone to talk to, talk to your friend Jesus!

*Lord, I thank You that You called me Your friend.
Give me the grace to develop my friendship with
You in Jesus' name.
Amen.*

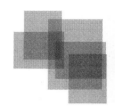

Day 57
He Lives in You!

*"But if the Spirit of Him who raised
Jesus from the dead dwells in you,
He who raised Christ from the dead
will also give life to your mortal bodies
through His Spirit who dwells in you."*

Romans 8:11

God Almighty lives on the inside of you. What the world says or thinks about you is irrelevant. What God says and thinks about you is relevant. You are a powerhouse.

Do not allow other people's opinions, your mistakes and what is going on in your life to become relevant. Allow God and His promises to become relevant in your life. He lives in you and He relates to you. Amen.

*Lord, I thank You that Your spirits resides in the
inside of me. Give me the grace to fully be tuned in
with Your spirit in the inside of me in Jesus' name.
Amen.*

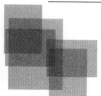

Simple and Powerful Truth to help Jump Start Your Day

Day 58
Trust in the Lord!

"Trust in the Lord with all your heart, and lean not on your own understanding; in all your ways acknowledge Him, And He shall direct your paths."

Proverbs 3:5-6

Having done all that you know to do, now is the time to trust in the Lord. Don't focus on how difficult things are. Every morning say to yourself, "I trust in You with all my heart. Give me the grace to enjoy the benefits of today." My friend, God will not fail or disappoint you. Trust in Him. Amen.

Lord, give me the grace to completely trust in You
in Jesus' name.
Amen.

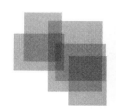

Day 59
He Will Complete!

*"Being confident of this very thing,
that He who has begun a good
work in you will complete it..."*

Philippians 1:6

God has begun His good work in the different areas of your life.
He promises to complete His work. Where you are right now is temporary.
God's good work is taking place in your life. You might not see the good
work of God, but God is working behind the scenes of your life making
crooked ways straight, restoring health and breathing His life into you.
Amen.

*Lord, I thank You for completing the good work You
began in every area of my life. Give me the grace to
continue to trust in You in Jesus' name.
Amen.*

_____

_____

_____

_____

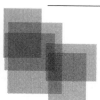

Simple and Powerful Truth to help Jump Start Your Day

Day 60
Fight!

"The Lord will fight for you, and
you shall hold your peace."

Exodus 14:14

Do not give up – fight! Fight for your marriage, fight for your children, fight for your life, health, finances and fight to win that situation confronting you. You are not fighting alone; God is fighting your battles for you. He already declares you victorious. The enemy has been defeated. The enemy of debt, loneliness, depression, sickness and your relationships has been defeated. Fight by praising God for your victory. Amen.

Lord, I thank You for fighting my battles for me.
May Your praises never cease in my life in Jesus'
name. Amen.

_____

_____

_____

_____

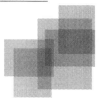

Day 61
Coming Together

"And we know that all things work together for good to those who love God, to those who are the called according to His purpose."

Romans 8:28

Not all things are for the good, but God can make a testimony out of your mess. He can make testimonies out of your tests, trials and tribulations; all things are coming together in your favor. You will overcome what was meant to destroy you. You are on your way to victories and breakthroughs; God is about to put the last pieces of the puzzle together concerning your situation. Rejoice, because your victories are in sight. Amen.

Lord, I thank You for causing all things to work together for my good. I give You praise in Jesus' name.
Amen.

_____

_____

_____

_____

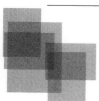

Simple and Powerful Truth to help Jump Start Your Day

Day 62
Glory of His Grace!

"To the praise of the glory of His grace, by which He made us accepted in the Beloved."

Ephesians 1:6

You are the object of God's glory, and He wants the glory (magnificence, splendor, beauty, wonder, grandeur, brilliance, exaltation, credit, fame and praise) of His grace (elegance, refinement, loveliness, polish, kindness and unmerited favor) to overflow in your life. God wants to magnify His goodness, glory and grace through you. Do not ever look down on yourself; you are approved, loved and accepted. Amen.

Lord, I thank You for the glory of Your grace in my life. Give me the grace to live in the fullness of the glory of Your grace in Jesus' name.
Amen.

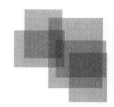

Day 63
You're Worthy!

*"Through the Lord's mercies we
are not consumed, Because His
compassions fail not. They are new
every morning; Great is
Your faithfulness."*

Lamentations 3:22-23

I was praying one morning and I said, "God, I am not worthy to come into
your presence..." Immediately, I heard a small voice that said to me,
"You are worthy, and I love you." My friend, you are worthy to our God.
There is nothing you can do to make Him love you less. You are the
redeemed of the Lord. He loves you, He believes in you and He wants the
best for you. When you are unfaithful, He is always faithful. Don't run
away from God; run to Him. You're worthy!

*Lord, I thank You for You calling me worthy in spite
of my unfaithfulness. Give me the grace to live
worthy life in Jesus' name.
Amen.*

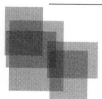

68

Day 64
Wonderfully Made

*"I will praise You, for I am
fearfully and wonderfully made;
Marvelous are Your works, And
that my soul knows very well."*

Psalms 139:14

Do not look down on yourself, do not allow what other people say, do or think about you to make you feel less. Our Aba Father masterfully and wonderfully made you.

You have the seed of greatness in the inside of you; you are made in the image of God. You are wonderful; you have what it takes in you to succeed. You have it in you to win. You are wonderfully made. Amen.

*Lord, give me the grace to recognize the greatness
on the inside of me and give me the grace to use it
to benefit others in Jesus' name.
Amen.*

_____

_____

_____

_____

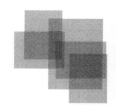

Day 65
He is Different!

" 'For My thoughts are not your
thoughts, Nor are your ways
My ways, ' says the Lord. "

Isaiah 55:8

We are limited in our thinking and in our ways. God is infinite in His thinking and in His ways. God has not run out of options concerning your finances, health, marriage, children and that situation confronting you. He knows what He's doing, He knows about that situation and He knows the best way for you. Keep doing your best and stop trying to figure things out. Trust in Him. Amen.

Lord, give me the grace to trust in You to do it Your
way in Jesus' name.
Amen.

_____

_____

_____

_____

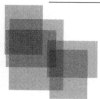

Simple and Powerful Truth to help Jump Start Your Day

Day 66
God Is with You!

"Have I not commanded you?
Be strong and courageous.
Do not be frightened, and do not
be dismayed, for the Lord your
God is with you wherever you go."

Joshua 1:9

God is going before you, He is going behind you, He is by your side and He lives in the inside of you. When you are asleep, He watches over you and He gives His angels charge over you. God is with you at all times. Allow the reality that God is with you to be dominant in your life and in your thoughts. You can trust our God to make a way, to deliver, to prosper, to set you free, to heal and to restore, because He is with you. Amen.

Lord, I thank You that You are with me. Give me
the grace to be strong and courageous in every
area of my life in Jesus' name.
Amen.

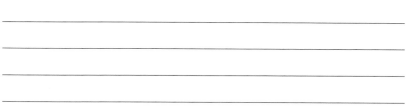

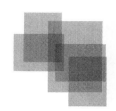

Day 67
Victory to Victory

*"But thanks be to God,
who gives us the victory through
our Lord Jesus Christ."*

1 Corinthians 15:57

You are not designed to have a moment of victory; you are designed to have victory to victory in every area of your life. The enemy has been defeated, and nothing can hold you back. Believe and declare victory over that situation. You are bound to have victory over that situation. Shout for victory and expect victory in your life today. Victory is yours. Amen.

*Lord, I receive Your victory in every area of my life.
I declare victory is mine in Jesus' name.
Amen*

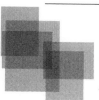

Simple and Powerful Truth to help Jump Start Your Day

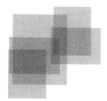

Day 68
Perfect Peace

"You will keep him in perfect peace, whose mind is stayed on You, because he trusts in You."

Isaiah 26:3

If you focus your mind on that situation, peace will be far away from you. No matter how challenging that situation is, God will give you the grace to overcome. When you worry, you lose; when you trust in God, you have peace. I pray for the grace to keep your mind stayed on God. Perfect peace is yours. Amen.

Lord, give me the grace to trust in You, and I thank You for keeping me in Your perfect peace in Jesus' name.
Amen.

_____

_____

_____

_____

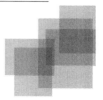

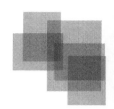

Day 69
New Things

"Do not remember the former things,
nor consider the things of old. Behold,
I will do a new thing, now it shall spring
forth; shall you not know it?
I will even make a road in the
wilderness and rivers in the desert."

Isaiah 43:18-19

God is doing new things in your life that will supersede your expectations. He is doing new things in your health, finances, relationships and family. He's opening new doors of opportunities for you. Live your life daily with the expectation of the new things of God becoming reality in your life. Amen.

Lord, I thank You for doing new things in every area
of my life. I declare I will experience the
super abundance and Your goodness in my life
in Jesus' name.
Amen

_____

_____

_____

_____

Simple and Powerful Truth to help Jump Start Your Day

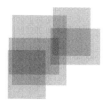

Day 70
You're Free!

"Therefore if the Son makes you free, you shall be free indeed."

John 8:36

Because you are in Christ, you have been set free from death to life, from sin to righteousness, from poverty to prosperity, from debt to abundance, from sickness to health and from dull mind to the mind of Christ. You're free. Say this out loud: "I am free from debt, addiction, sickness, loneliness and depression." You're free in Jesus' name. Amen.

Lord, I receive Your freedom for every area
of my life. Every chain has been broken of you
in Jesus' name.
Amen.

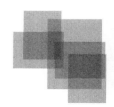

Day 71
Draw Near!

"Draw near to God and
He will draw near to you..."

James 4:8

Draw near to God, the source of everything you need, not to your problem. Don't claim your problems; claim the promises of God concerning every area of your life.

When you draw near to God in the midst of that difficult situation through prayers, praises and thanksgivings, He will draw near to you with deliverance, freedom, peace and abundance. Draw near to God, and He will draw near to you. Amen.

Lord,
give me the grace to draw near to you at all times
in Jesus' name.
Amen.

Simple and Powerful Truth to help Jump Start Your Day

Day 72
Strength

*"...For the joy of the Lord
is your strength."*

Nehemiah 8:10

The joy of the Lord is your strength, and the enemy is after the joy of
the Lord in your life. He wants you to focus on that situation, because
he knows that it will drain the joy of the Lord in your life. Don't let him.
Instead focus on God and give Him praise for your victory. Amen.

Lord, I thank You that Your joy is my strength.
I give You praise for my victory in Jesus' name.
Amen

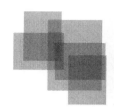

Day 73
Be Quick!

"Be sober, be vigilant;
because your adversary the devil
walks about like a roaring lion,
seeking whom he may devour."

1 Peter 5:8

Be quick to reject, refuse and rebuke the enemy in your life. The enemy is a deceiver, magnifier, accuser and instigator. He does all these through filling your mind with thoughts of defeat. He will suggest that you will never make it, overcome that addiction, get out of debit or get well. Instead of dwelling on those thoughts, be quick to reject them. Declare that you are a victor, above not beneath, blessed, an overcomer full of God's amazing grace. Amen.

Lord, give me the grace to be sober, vigilant and
quick to rebuke the devil in every area of my life
in Jesus' name.
Amen.

_____

_____

_____

_____

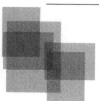

Simple and Powerful Truth to help Jump Start Your Day

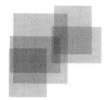

Day 74
Twice as Much

"...Indeed the Lord gave Job
twice as much as he had before."

Job 42:10

The Lord will give you twice as much. He will give you double for your trouble. He will give you twice the peace, joy, wisdom, protection, abundance, and twice the godly relationships. He will open twice as many doors of opportunities for you. Your sorrow, frustrations, lacks and troubles are coming to an end. My friend, get ready for twice as much of God's goodness in every area of your life. Amen.

Lord, I thank You for twice as much of
Your goodness in every area of my life in Jesus'
name. Amen.

_____

_____

_____

_____

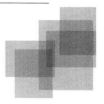

Day 75
Two, Together

*"Again I say to you that if two
of you agree on earth concerning
anything that they ask,
it will be done for them by
My Father in heaven."*

Matthew 18:19

The verse above says if two or more are in agreement on one thing, it will be done for us. I join my faith with yours and I agree with you that you will overcome that situation. I am in agreement with you for an increase of God's favor in your life. I am also in agreement for your freedom, good health, abundance and breakthroughs. Your mouth shall be filled with the testimonies of God's faithfulness in Jesus' name. Amen.

*I agree with you that God will do abundantly,
above and beyond all that you are asking and
believing for in every area of your life
in Jesus' name.
Amen.*

_____

_____

_____

_____

Simple and Powerful Truth to help Jump Start Your Day

Day 76
The Same Spirit

"But if the Spirit of Him who raised Jesus from the dead dwells in you, He who raised Christ from the dead will also give life to your mortal bodies through His Spirit who dwells in you."

Romans 8:11

The same Spirit that raised Christ from the dead dwells on the inside of you. You are a powerhouse, and God Almighty is the source of your power. Christ dwells in you and He is greater than anything confronting you. Don't allow that situation to create fear in you; let the reality of Christ dwelling in you inspire faith in you to overcome. Amen.

I decree and declare that every dead thing in your finances, health and in your relationships is been raised back to life; you will rise up with praise shouting for joy in Jesus' name.
Amen.

_____

_____

_____

_____

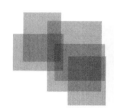

Day 77
This is the Day!

*"This is the day the Lord
has made; we will rejoice and
be glad in it."*

Psalms 118:24

This is the day that Lord has made personally for you. You have every reason to rejoice and be glad in today, because it's the day that the Lord has made for you. God doesn't make junk. There are many goods available for you today. Lay aside every worry, fear, insufficiency and doubt and focus on the goodness of God today. Amen.

> *Lord, I lift my up hands to heaven and thank You for this beautiful day in spite of what is going on in your life. I thank You that Your favor will overflow in my life in Jesus' name*
> *Amen.*

_____

_____

_____

_____

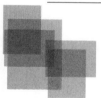

Day 78
Rejoicing in Hope

"Rejoicing in hope,
patient in tribulation,
continuing steadfastly in prayer."

Romans 12:12

Rejoice in hope, knowing fully well that God is faithful, that He will fulfill His promises in your life. Rejoice in hope, be patient in your believing and keep on giving thanks to God for your victory. Put your hope in God and continue to do your best. Most importantly, continue to rejoice in hope not for the pain but because God is on your side and He is faithful. Amen.

Lord, give me the grace to consistently rejoice
in hope in Jesus' name.
Amen.

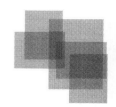

Day 79
They're Broken

"You have broken down all his hedges; You have brought his strongholds to ruin."

Psalms 89:40

I declare that every stronghold of addiction, sickness, debt, depression, worries and lack are broken in the name of Jesus. They are broken, and I declare victory, freedom, peace, joy and abundance over your life. You are favored, blessed and abounding in the grace of God. Believe it and receive it in Jesus' name. Amen.

Lord, I receive Your victory into every area of my life
in Jesus' name.
Amen.

_____

_____

_____

_____

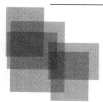

Simple and Powerful Truth to help Jump Start Your Day

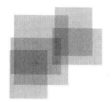

Day 80
Every Reason

"In God we boast all day long,
and praise Your name forever."

Psalms 44:8

Today and before this week is over, you will have every reason to give thanks to God. Your mouth shall be filled with praise. Live today expecting the favor of God to abound in your life. You're blessed and highly favored. Amen.

Lord, I thank You that You will give me something
to talk about in Jesus' name.
Amen.

_____

_____

_____

_____

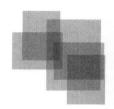

Day 81
Set Your Mind

*" Set your mind on things above,
not on things on the earth. "*

Colossians 3:2

Your life is affected by your dominant thoughts. When you set your mind on loving God and taking hold of His promises, eventually they will become reality in your life. Do not set your mind on that situation. Your mind will not set itself on loving God and on His promises. You have to intentionally set your mind to love, prayers, patience, favor, what God says about you and giving thanks. Amen.

*Lord, give me the grace to consistently set my mind
on You in Jesus' name.
Amen.*

Simple and Powerful Truth to help Jump Start Your Day

Day 82
Showers of Blessings

"Be glad then, you children of Zion, and rejoice in the Lord your God; For He has given you the former rain faithfully, And He will cause the rain to come down for you – the former rain, and the latter rain in the first month."

Joel 2:23

There shall be showers of blessing, and your sorrows are coming to an end. The things you have struggled with, you will do with ease. I declare peace, joy, favor, protection, wisdom and sudden breakthroughs that will rain over your life. My friend, showers of blessings are coming your way! Amen.

Lord, I thank You for Your showers of blessings overflowing in my life in Jesus' name.
Amen.

Day 83
Submit to Him!

"Therefore submit to God.
Resist the devil and
he will flee from you. "

James 4:7 NKJV

The power of the enemy is no match to the power of our God.
When you submit to God by trusting in Him, by praising Him and by
declaring His promises over your life, you are resisting the devil,
and he will flee from you.

I declare that the enemy will flee from your health,
marriage and finances, from your children,
from your business and from every area of your life.
Keep praising God for your victory in Jesus' name.
Amen.

Simple and Powerful Truth to help Jump Start Your Day

Day 84
He Died for You!

"Beloved, I pray that you may prosper in all things and be in health, just as your soul prospers."

3 John 1:2

Jesus Christ died for you so that you can live. He died for your sins, so you can become righteous; He died for your freedom, prosperity, for your healing. He died for everything that you will ever need for in every area of your life. He died for you. He died for that situation confronting you. Lift Him up today and know that He died for you and He is alive and alive on the inside of you.

Lord, give me the grace to enjoy the fullness of Your blessings that You died to give me in Jesus' name. Amen.

_____

_____

_____

_____

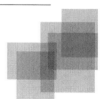

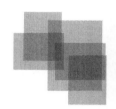

Day 85
It's All About Him!

" 'I am the Alpha and the Omega,
the Beginning and the End,'
says the Lord, 'who is and who was
and who is to come, the Almighty.' "

Revelation 1:8

When you make everything about Him, He will make everything about you. As a matter of fact, He already made everything about you when He sent His only begotten son to die for you. When you lift Him up, He will lift away the situation confronting you. He loves you and He wants the best for you. It's all about Him. Do not focus on the situation confronting you; make everything about Him. Amen.

Lord, give me the grace to make everything about
You in Jesus' name.
Amen

_____

_____

_____

_____

Simple and Powerful Truth to help Jump Start Your Day

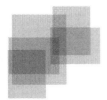

Day 86
He Will Repay

"Beloved, do not avenge
yourselves, but rather give place
to wrath; for it is written,
'Vengeance is Mine, I will repay,'
says the Lord."

Romans 12:19

God is fighting your battles for you and He is your vindicator. People might betray you, talk bad about you, or hurt you; do not try to get even. The Lord will repay and give you double for your trouble. He is not surprised about the mistreatment, hurt, betrayal and naysayers. Continue to be good to others and give Him thanks; He will repay you for all you have endured. Amen.

Lord, give me the grace to trust in You to be my
vindicator in Jesus' name.
Amen.

Day 87
Stop Worrying!

"Let not your heart be troubled;
you believe in God,
believe also in me."

John 14:1

Stop worrying about that situation. Worrying produces negative results and stops you from moving your life forward. It takes away your ability to focus on God, your helper. God is telling you to stop worrying and He is giving you an incredible invitation to believe in Him to turn that situation around. Stop worrying and start praising God for your breakthroughs. Amen.

Lord, give me the grace to stop worrying and start
praising You for turning things around in my favor
in Jesus' name.
Amen.

_____

_____

_____

_____

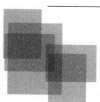

Simple and Powerful Truth to help Jump Start Your Day

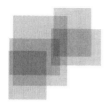

Day 88
God of Hope

*"Now may the God of hope fill
you with all joy and peace in
believing, that you may abound in
hope by
the power of the Holy Spirit."*

Romans 15:13

Trusting and believing during difficult times can be challenging, but the God of hope will fill your heart with joy and peace and in your believing He will cause you to abound in hope. You are not going under, you are going over the top. Amen.

*I pray that the God of hope will fill your heart with
much joy and peace for believing. Hope will rise
up on the inside of you in Jesus' name.
Amen.*

_____

_____

_____

_____

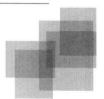

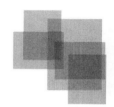

Day 89
Grace of Our Lord

*"The grace of our Lord Jesus
Christ be with you. Amen."*

1 Thessalonians 5:28

The grace of our Lord will cause you to triumph, to overcome, to have breakthroughs and to shout for joy. I declare that the grace of God is with you in every area of your life and causes you to abound in the fullness of His goodness. Focus on His grace today. Amen.

*Lord, give me the grace to enjoy the full benefits
of Your grace in Jesus' name.
Amen.*

Day 90
Madly in Love

*"For his anger endures but a
moment; in his favor is life:
weeping may endure for a night,
but joy comes in the morning."*

Psalms 30:5

I want you to know that God is not mad at you; he is madly in love with
you. There is nothing you can do to make Him love you less. In spite of
what is going on in your life, His desire for you is to have enough favor
and restoration and become an overcomer. Your Aba Father, who is madly
in love with you, will cause you to be victorious. Amen.

*Lord, I thank You for turning my mourning into
dancing and my sorrow into joy in Jesus' name.
Amen.*

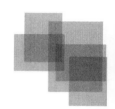

Day 91
Sworn Blessings

" 'By Myself I have sworn,' says the Lord 'because you have done this thing, and have not withheld your son, your only son... blessing I will bless you, and multiplying I will multiply your descendants...' "

Genesis 22:16-17

God is determined to bless you. He swore to bless you and do for you what you can't do in your own power. Keep on trusting, believing, giving and declaring His promises over your life. That situation is no match for our God. He swore to bless and multiply His blessings in your life. Hope and trust in Him today. Amen.

Lord, give me the grace to believe, honor You with my life and receive Your blessings in every area of my life in Jesus' name.
Amen.

_____

_____

_____

_____

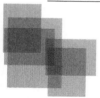

Simple and Powerful Truth to help Jump Start Your Day

Day 92
Glory to Glory

"But we all, with unveiled face,
beholding as in a mirror the glory
of the Lord, are being transformed
into the same image from glory
to glory, just as by the
Spirit of the Lord."

2 Corinthians 3:18

My friend, you have total access to God through our Lord Jesus Christ. Through Him you can go to God 24/7. The more you go to Him in prayer and praise, the more your life will be transformed from glory to glory. Go to God today concerning your life and that situation confronting you and watch your life and that situation transform from glory to glory. Amen.

I declare you will move from glory to glory in your
health, relationships, finances and in every area of
your life in Jesus' name.
Amen

_____

_____

_____

_____

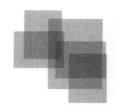

Day 93
Liberty

"Now the Lord is the Spirit;
and where the Spirit of the Lord is,
there is liberty."

2 Corinthians 3:17

The Spirit of the Lord is in the inside of you. When you allow the Spirit, He will lead you, guide you, and inspire you in every affair of life. Because the Spirit of the Lord is in you, you have access to liberty. I pray that you will have the grace to develop your relationship with the Spirit of the Lord on the inside of you. Amen.

I declare liberty from sickness, pain, debt and
lack and from anything that is holding you back
in Jesus' name.
Amen.

98

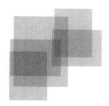

Day 94
Fortunes

*"Evil (misfortunes) pursues
sinners, but to the righteous, good
(fortunes) shall be repaid."*

Proverbs 13:21

As a believer in Christ you are made for success, abundance and prosperity
in every area of your life. I want to encourage you to a have fortune
mentality. You are designed for fortune, and your Heavenly Father owns it
all. Wealth is stored up for you. Believe it, take actions, claim it and declare
His promises over your life. Amen.

*Lord, give me the grace to have a fortune
mentality in every area of my life in Jesus' name.
Amen.*

Day 95
Partner with God

*"Commit your works to the Lord,
and your thoughts will
be established."*

Proverbs 16:3

God wants to be your partner in small and in big things of life. Commit your plans, work and life to God and wholly trust in Him, and He will cause your thoughts to become agreeable to His will and your plan to be established and succeed. Instead of trying to figure everything out, partner with God.
He knows all things. Amen.

*Lord, give me the grace to commit my work and my
life consistently to You in Jesus' name.
Amen.*

_____

_____

_____

_____

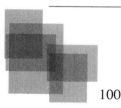

Simple and Powerful Truth to help Jump Start Your Day

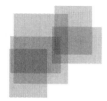

Day 96
First Thing First

"But seek first the kingdom of
God and His righteousness,
and all these things shall
be added to you."

Matthew 6:33

Your success in life can be summed up in whom and what you sought after.
First thing first, seek after God on a daily basis. He will guide, provide
favor, lead, make a way for you, heal you and protect you. He will restore
joy, peace and broken relationships. He will multiply your time, your
money and your wisdom. First thing first! Amen.

Lord, give me the grace to seek after Your kingdom
in every area of my life in Jesus' name.
Amen.

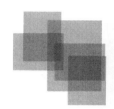

Day 97
He's Your Peace!

"Be anxious for nothing, but in everything by prayer and supplication, with thanksgiving, let your requests be made known to God; and the peace of God, which surpasses all understanding, will guard your hearts and minds through Christ Jesus."

Philippians 4:6-7

How can you be worry-free and full of peace in the midst of difficult situations? By making your request known to God through prayers and thanksgiving. When you pray and give thanks for your victory, you are saying, "God, I trust in You and I know that You will never fail me." He is your peace. Amen.

Lord, give me the grace to be anxious for nothing;
Cause me to make my request known to You through
prayers and thanksgivings in Jesus' name.
Amen.

_____

_____

_____

_____

Simple and Powerful Truth to help Jump Start Your Day

Day 98
Never Condemned

"There is therefore now no condemnation to those who are in Christ Jesus..."

Romans 8:1

God loves you unconditionally and He can never condemn you.
Your mistakes, sins and failures are no match for the grace and the mercy
of God. Stop beating yourself up, get back up and know today that you can
never be condemned. You are loved. Praise God! Amen.

Give me the grace to live my life free of
condemnation. I thank You for Your righteousness
in my life in Jesus' name.
Amen.

_____

_____

_____

_____

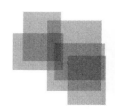

Day 99
The Lord of Hosts!

"Then David said to the Philistine,
'You come to me with a sword, with a
spear, and with a javelin. But I come to
you in the name of the LORD OF HOSTS,
the God of the armies of Israel,
whom you have defied.'"

1 Samuel 17:45

Are you confronted with a difficult situation? Is something or someone troubling your spirit? Do not go in your strength to confronting that situation; go in the name of the LORD OF HOSTS. David did and he defeated Goliath. Declare, in the name of the Lord of hosts, depression, anger, jealousy, lack, marriage trouble, confusion and sickness are gone from your life and family. Amen

Lord, be the LORD OF HOSTS over my family,
finances, health, relationships and over every area of
my life in Jesus' name.
Amen.

_____

_____

_____

_____

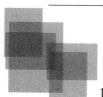

104

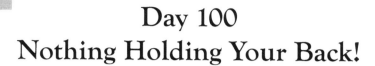

Day 100
Nothing Holding Your Back!

"He brought them out of darkness
and the shadow of death,
and broke their chains in pieces."

Psalms 107:14

You are a child of God, and nothing can hold you back from experiencing the fullness of God in your life. I declare that chains are broken off of you; I declare freedom from whatever and whoever is holding you back in Jesus' name. Display a mentality of freedom and do not allow anything to hold you back. Amen.

Lord, I thank You for bringing me out of darkness
into Your marvelous light. I thank you for breaking
chains that are holding me back in every area of
my life in Jesus' name.
Amen.

_____

_____

_____

_____

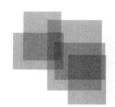

Day 101
Keep Your Heart!

"Keep your heart (mind) with all diligence, for out of it spring the issues of life."

Proverbs 4:23

Everything matters: what you listen to, read, watch, and whom you associate with.

Everything rises and falls on the condition of your mind. Keep your mind with all diligence, because life flows from it. Set your heart on His promises. Amen.

Lord, give me the grace to keep my heart (mind)
with all diligence. Have Your way in my life
in Jesus' name.
Amen.

_____

_____

_____

_____

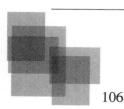

Simple and Powerful Truth to help Jump Start Your Day

Day 102
Think on God's Thoughts

"Finally, brethren, whatever things are true...noble... just... pure...lovely... good report, if there is any virtue and if there is anything praiseworthy —meditate on these things."

Philippians 4:8

You win or lose the battle in your mind. It's easy to think bad thoughts when confronted with a difficult situation. What will cause you to triumph is thinking and dwelling on the promises of God. Your dominant thoughts will determine the course of your life. Think on God's thoughts! Amen.

Lord, give me the grace to think and focus on Your promises for every area of my life in Jesus' name. Amen.

_____

_____

_____

_____

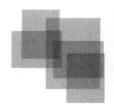

Day 103
Man of War!

"The Lord is a man of war;
The Lord is His name."

Exodus 15:3

Whatever is coming against you is coming against God. Our God is a man of war and He will fight your battles for you. You need to fully comprehend that the Lord is on your side. The enemy wants you to magnify your fear and that situation confronting you, instead of magnifying God, the man of war that already declared you victorious. Trust in Him today. Amen.

Lord, give me the grace to magnify You more than
the problem confronting me. I thank You for fighting
my battles for me in Jesus' name.
Amen.

_____

_____

_____

_____

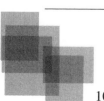

Simple and Powerful Truth to help Jump Start Your Day

Day 104
Due Season

"And let us not grow weary while doing good, for in due season we shall reap if we do not lose heart."

Galatians 6:9

Have you been praying about a situation? Believing, giving, trusting, yet you see little or no resolve? Do not give up; you are closer than you think. At just the right time, in due season, you will reap a harvest of blessings. Maybe you feel weary, but arise, receive His grace and move forward. You will not miss your due season. Amen.

Lord, give me the grace not to grow weary in doing good in Jesus' name.
Amen.

_____

_____

_____

_____

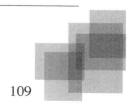

Day 105
The Wise

"The wise man store for the future, but the foolish man spends whatever he gets."

Proverbs 21:20

How do you determine a wise person? They do not spend everything they earn. Be wise – prepare for the future so you do not have to worry about the future. Give thanks for the future, declare your victory for the future, love for the future and learn for the future. Leave a legacy! Amen.

I pray that God will give you the grace and the wisdom to store up for the future in Jesus' name.
Amen.

_____

_____

_____

_____

Simple and Powerful Truth to help Jump Start Your Day

Day 106
Pursue Righteousness

*"He who pursues righteousness
and love finds life, prosperity
and honor."*

Proverbs 21:21

The wise pursue righteousness and love. They know they will find life, prosperity and honor in every area of their lives. You do not have to be perfect to be pure when your mind is set on living your life to honor God. He will give you the grace to live a holy life. Amen.

*Lord, give me the grace to live a righteous life.
I thank You for prosperity and honor in every area
of my life in Jesus' name.
Amen*

_____

_____

_____

_____

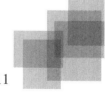

Day 107
The Keys

"I will give you the keys of the kingdom of heaven, and whatever you bind on earth will be bound in heaven, and whatever you loose on earth will be loosed in heaven."

Matthew16:19

God has given you the keys to good health, abundance, wisdom and authority over every evil force. Whatever you bind in any area of your life will be bound in heaven. Whatever you lose in any area of your life will be loosened in heaven. You are a powerhouse. Don't allow that situation to reduce you to nothing. Arise and use the keys. Amen.

Lord, give me the grace to grow in the authority
You have given to me. I receive Your grace to bind
anything that is coming against me and the grace
to loose your blessings into every area of my life in
Jesus' name.
Amen.

_____

_____

_____

_____

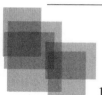

Simple and Powerful Truth to help Jump Start Your Day

Day 108
The Faithful!

"A faithful man will abound
with blessings..."

Proverbs 28:20

Being faithful does not mean you do not make mistakes. It is about who you are and who you are is not perfect. Have a mindset of faithfulness and when you are unfaithful God is still faithful. Get back up and get back into faithfulness. Many blessings to you today! Amen.

Lord, give me the grace to be faithful in all
circumstances in Jesus' name.
Amen.

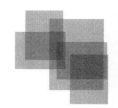

Day 109
Sow Your Seed!

*"In the morning sow your seed,
and in the evening do not withhold
your hand; for you do not know
which will prosper, either this
or that, Or whether both alike
will be good."*

Ecclesiastes 11:6

Take the focus off of you and that situation; instead focus on seed sowing opportunities. Your harvest of peace, joy, health, favor, wisdom, and prosperity are in sight. Remember the saying, "What you make happen for others, God will make happen for you." Amen.

*Lord, give me the grace to be a master seed sower
in Jesus' name.
Amen.*

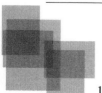

114

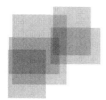

Day 110
Good Treasures

*"A good man out of the good
treasure of his heart brings forth
good things, and an evil man
out of the evil treasure brings
forth evil things."*

Matthew12:35

The dominant thoughts in your mind will determine your reality.
The problem is not the problem; your perception of the problem is the
problem. Feed your mind with the thoughts of victory and breakthrough.
Build up the good treasures in your heart; they will come in handy in
times of need. Amen.

*Lord, give me the grace to store up good treasure
in my mind in Jesus' name.
Amen.*

_____

_____

_____

_____

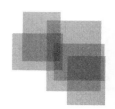

Day 111
His Plan

*"For I know the thoughts that
I think toward you, says the Lord,
thoughts of peace and not of evil,
to give you a future and a hope."*

Jeremiah 29:11

Know that God has your best interest at heart. His plan for your life is peace not evil, health not sickness, abundance not lacks and joy not sorrow. God is thinking good thoughts about you. With our God, your future is bright in spite of that situation. Get back up, get going and get ready for a big celebration of your breakthrough. It's not over. Amen.

*Lord, I pray that Your plan for my life will be
fulfilled. Protect me from distractions and give the
wisdom to make wise decisions in Jesus' name.
Amen.*

Simple and Powerful Truth to help Jump Start Your Day

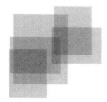

Day 112
Call on God!

"Call to Me,
and I will answer you,
and show you great and mighty
things, which you do not know."

Jeremiah 33:3

God is your everything, and He wants you to call on Him concerning that situation. He is interested in you, and you can never be a burden to Him. Instead of worrying, call on God, and He will answer you. He will show up and do great and mighty things in your life. He is the answer to that situation. Call on Him and give thanks for your victory. Amen.

Lord, give me the grace to call on You at all times.
I praise You for Your goodness in my life in Jesus' name.
Amen.

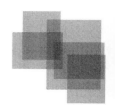

Day 113
Signs

*"And these signs will follow those who believe:
In My name they will cast out demons;
they will speak with new tongues; they will
take up serpents; and if they drink anything
deadly, it will by no means hurt them; they will
lay hands on the sick, and they will recover."*

Mark 16:17-18

You have it in you to win. God placed Himself on the inside of you.
Lord, I thank You for the power you have given me over sicknesses,
diseases, demons and for the power to overcome in every area of my life.
Help me to fully comprehend this power in order to use it in overcome
every area of my life. Amen.

*I declare that I am anointed, full of power and full
of God's grace, and no weapon formed against me
shall prosper in Jesus' name.*
Amen.

_____

_____

_____

_____

Simple and Powerful Truth to help Jump Start Your Day

Day 114
He Came To Bless You

*"The thief does not come except
to steal, and to kill, and to destroy.
I have come that they may have
life, and that they may have it
more abundantly."*

John 10:10

Lord, I thank You for the abundant life You came to give to me. Help me to enjoy it to the fullest. Give me the wisdom and creative ways to maximize abundant living in every area of my life. Open my eyes to see the tricks of the devil and give me the grace to overcome them in Jesus' name. Amen.

*Lord, I receive the abundant life You came to give
in every area of my life. Give me the grace to have
an abundant mentality in Jesus' name.
Amen.*

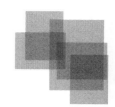

Day 115
Pay Attention!

*"Watch and pray, lest you enter
into temptation. The spirit indeed is
willing, but the flesh is weak."*

Matthew 26:41

When I reflect back to my life, all my mistakes and failures happened for lack of paying attention. I was not paying attention; as a result, I failed and made a series of stupid mistakes. Thank God for restoration! Watch and pray and pay attention to every aspect of your life so that life will not catch you by surprise. Amen.

*Lord, give me the grace to watch and pray. Help me to
pay attention to every aspect of my life in Jesus' name.
Amen*

Simple and Powerful Truth to help Jump Start Your Day

Day 116
The Same Thing

"No temptation has overtaken you except such as is common to man; but God is faithful, who will not allow you to be tempted beyond what you are able, but with the temptation will also make the way of escape, that you may be able to bear it."

1 Corinthians 10:13

All of us will be tempted in different ways by people and through different situations. But you can overcome any temptation, trials and tribulations through the grace of God. Give up the excuses and take on the grace of God to overcome. Ask God to help you overcome, and He will. Amen.

Lord, give me the grace to overcome any temptation. I choose to honor You with my life in Jesus' name. Amen.

_____

_____

_____

_____

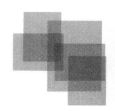

Day 117
God Is for You

"What then shall we say to these things? If God is for us, who can be against us?"

Romans 8:31

God is your friend, provider, healer, protector, wisdom and everything. God is for you and He is on your side; He is fighting your battles for you and making a way for you, where there seems to be no way. He is for you and no one, situation, sickness or disease can be against you. No financial issue, demon, or evil can be against you. Believe and receive this into your heart today. Amen.

Lord, I thank You for You are for me and I thank You that no weapon formed against me that shall prosper and Thank that by Your grace I'm victorious in Jesus' name.
Amen.

_____

_____

_____

_____

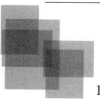

Simple and Powerful Truth to help Jump Start Your Day

Day 118
Never Alone

*"He Himself has said, 'I will
never leave you nor forsake you.'
So we may boldly say: 'The Lord
is my helper; I will not fear.
What can man do to me?'"*

Hebrews 13:5-6

You are never alone. God is in you. He is on your side; He is with you,
He is going before you, and you are the apple of His eye. You might feel
lonely, but you are never alone, and He understands your pain. Shake
off that loneliness, depression, fear and condemnation. The Lord is your
helper and He is fighting your battles for you, in the midst of that situation.
Always say to yourself, "God is with me." Amen.

*Lord, give me the grace to not feel alone and
lonely. Give me the grace to rely on You, my helper
and my deliverer in Jesus' name.
Amen.*

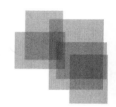

Day 119
Don't Worry!

"Let not your heart be troubled;
you believe in God,
believe also in me."

John 14:1

What situations are you worried about? Don't worry; it stops you from moving forward in a positive direction. Worrying takes away your ability to focus on God, your Helper. Focus on what you have control over and begin to take baby steps to your breakthroughs. Don't worry; believe in God your provider, helper, vindicator and your deliverer. Amen.

Lord, give me the grace to not worry.
Cause me to trust in You in Jesus' name.
Amen.

_____

_____

_____

_____

Simple and Powerful Truth to help Jump Start Your Day

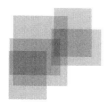

Day 120
Be Nice to You

"And be kind to one another, tenderhearted, forgiving one another, even as God in Christ forgave you."

Ephesians 4:32

Be nice to you; let go of the hurt, pain, disappointment and betrayal by others. Human beings have the capacity to inflict all the above, but God has the capacity to heal, restore and rejuvenate your life. Forgiveness is for you; it brings healing, rest, peace, energy and control over your life. When you forgive, you are reflecting the character of God. Amen.

Lord, give me the grace to be kind and
tenderhearted and to forgive.
I release my hurt, pain, disappointment and
betrayal to You and I receive Your joy and peace
for my life in Jesus' name.
Amen.

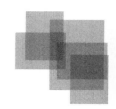

Day 121
Don't Give Up!

"Count it all joy when you fall into various trials, knowing that the testing of your faith produces patience. But let patience have its perfect work, that you may be perfect and complete, lacking nothing."

James 1:3-4

We have all heard the saying, "When you are down to nothing, God is up to something." Every difficulty, disappointment, rejection and failure has an equivalent opportunity that comes along with it.
Do not give up; you are closer to your victory than you think. You cannot make up for five years of mistakes in five days; be patient with the process of transformation in your life. It is well.

Lord, fill my heart with Your joy all the time.
Give me the grace to not give up in the face of
difficulty in Jesus name.
Amen.

_____

_____

_____

_____

Simple and Powerful Truth to help Jump Start Your Day

Day 122
Your Dream Team

"Two are better than one,
because they have a good reward
for their labor. For if they fall,
one will lift up his companion..."

Ecclesiastes 4:9-10

No one is an island. Each and every one of us needs people that can carry us along during difficult times in our lives. Having a team of people around you is very important. Have your dream team for your life; they will keep you accountable, keep you on course, love you, correct you, inspire you and cheer you up. I pray for wisdom and guidance in selecting your dream team. Amen.

Lord, weed the wrong people out of my life and
bring the right people into my life. I pray for Your
divine connections. Give me the grace and the
wisdom to select my dream team in Jesus' name.
Amen.

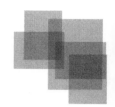

Day 123
Be Strong!

"Be strong and of good courage,
do not fear nor be afraid of THEM;
for the Lord your God, He is the
One who goes with you. He will not
leave you nor forsake you."

Deuteronomy 31:6

How strong are you when things are not going well, when you are faced with a difficult situation? Difficulty has the potential to drain your energy if you allow it. It is very easy to get discouraged and allow fear into your life when you go through a difficult situation. God is with you and He said He would never leave you or forsake you. Trust in Him to see you through. Be strong and never give up hope! Amen.

Lord, give me the grace to be strong and of good
courage. I receive Your boldness into my life
in Jesus' name.
Amen.

_____

_____

_____

_____

Simple and Powerful Truth to help Jump Start Your Day

Day 124
The Perfect Maker

"The Lord will perfect that
which concerns me..."

Psalms 138:8

Our God is a faithful God and He desires to make your life better every day.

He said He will perfect that which concerns you. Everything in your life concerns Him. If you have a health issue, He will perfect His healing in your body. If you have financial difficulty, He will perfect His abundance and give you wisdom for profitable endeavors. Know today that God is perfecting everything that concerns you. Amen.

Lord, I thank You that You are perfecting
everything that concerns me. Your favor,
health, abundance and everything that pertains life
and godliness are been perfected in my life
in Jesus' name.
Amen.

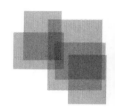

Day 125
Abide In Him

"If you abide in Me, and My words abide in you, you will ask what you desire, and it shall be done for you."

John 15:7

Do not abide in that situation, abide in God and let His word dwell in you. When you do, faith will rise up on the inside of you and causes you to ask what you desire in faith. When you allow God to be the center of your life and that situation, you will have proper desires for your life and faith to overcome that situation. Abide in Him and in His word. Amen.

Lord, give me the grace to abide in You and in Your word. Be the center of my life in Jesus' name. Amen.

Day 126
Walk by Faith

"For we walk
by faith, not by sight."

2 Corinthians 5:7

That situation might not make sense to you, but it makes sense to God, and He is not surprised by what you are going through. See yourself victorious through the eyes of faith; get the promises of God concerning that situation. Declare those promises over that situation and go about your day thanking God for your breakthrough. Amen.

Lord, give me the grace to walk by faith not
by sight. I thank You for Your victory and
breakthroughs in my life in Jesus' name.
Amen.

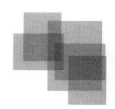

Day 127
Position Your Hope

"O Israel, hope in the Lord;
for with the Lord there is mercy,
and with Him is
abundant redemption."

Psalms 130:7

When you hope in someone or something, you have the expectation that hoping in that thing or that person will make your life better. Position your hope in God; He will never fail you. People have the potential to fail and disappoint you; do not place your hope in people. Hope in God who is faithful, full of mercy, love, wisdom and abundance. Say this out loud: "Lord, I hope in You." Amen.

Lord, give me the grace to position my hope in
You. I thank You for Your mercy and Your abundant
redemption in Jesus' name.
Amen.

_____

_____

_____

_____

132

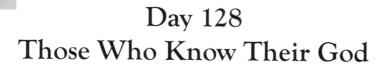

Day 128
Those Who Know Their God

*"...The people who know their
God shall be strong, and carry out
great exploits."*

Daniel 11:32

Those who know their God are strong, full of hope and favor-minded. Know today that God wants to be good to you; you are the apple of His eyes and you are engraved in the palms of His hands. He is faithful even when you are unfaithful and He loves you unconditionally. Know today that God is on your side; let hope rise in the inside of you. Amen.

*Lord, give me the grace to know You more and the
grace to make You known to others.
Use me for Your glory in Jesus' name.
Amen.*

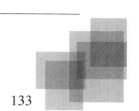

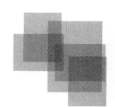

Day 129
Renewed Strength!

*"Those who wait on the Lord shall
renew their strength; they shall
mount up with wings like eagles,
they shall run and not be weary,
they shall walk and not faint."*

Isaiah 40:31

If you desire renewed strength, do not wait on your spouse, job, friends or the government. Wait on the Lord by worshipping with other believers, by putting your trust in Him, having patience, waiting in faith and having positive expectations. When you worship with other believers, faith and hope will rise up in the inside of you. Your strength will be renewed and you will mount up with the wings of eagles, living above the circumstances of life. Amen

*Lord, give me the grace to wait on You.
Have Your way in my life in Jesus' name.
Amen.*

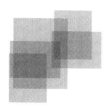

Day 130
Show Off

*"Then all this assembly shall
know that the Lord does not save
with sword and spear; for the
battle is the Lord's, and He will
give you into our hands."*

1 Samuel 17:47

God wants to display His glory through you. He wants to manifest His blessings, favor and goodness in your life. He wants to show off through you. He will defeat your enemy and cause you to be victorious. Your enemy is no match for our God. Remember this: God wants to make you a "show off" of His glorious grace. Amen.

*Lord, I thank You for making me the object of Your
glory. Show Your goodness through me in Jesus'
name. Amen.*

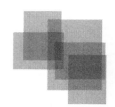

Day 131
Call on God

*"The righteous cry out, and the
Lord hears and delivers them out of
all their troubles..."*

Psalms 34:17

When going through difficult times, when faced with a difficult situation or person, develop the habit of calling on God first. When you call on God, He will answer you with hope, peace, joy, wisdom, grace, divine connection, protection, healing, favor and anything that would make your life better. Amen.

*Lord, give me the grace to call on You at all times in
Jesus' name.
Amen.*

Simple and Powerful Truth to help Jump Start Your Day

Day 132
Believe Immediately

"Whatever things you ask in
prayer, believing,
you will receive."

Matthew 21:27

When you ask God in prayer for anything, believe immediately and keep on believing that you receive what you asked God for in your prayers. Have a vision of what you asked God for ingrained in your mind. See yourself healed, delivered, blessed, restored, favored and hunger and thirsty after righteousness. Amen.

> *Lord, give me the grace to continue believing in*
> *You until Your promises become reality in my life*
> *in Jesus' name.*
> *Amen.*

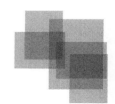

Day 133
Encamped

*"The angel of the Lord encamps
all around those who fear Him,
and delivers them."*

Psalms 34:7

Know today that God has assigned His angels to encamp around you.
You are not alone; God is in the inside of you. He is going before you,
He is by your side and He has assigned His angels to encamp around you.
You have the divine protection of God; the angel of the Lord encamps
all around your house, marriage, children, family and everything about
your life. Amen.

*Lord, I thank You for encamping Your angel around
me. Give me the grace to live my life to honor You
in Jesus' name.
Amen*

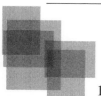

Simple and Powerful Truth to help Jump Start Your Day

Day 134
Words

*"Let no corrupt word proceed out
of your mouth, but what is good
for necessary edification, that it
may impart grace to the hearers."*

Ephesians 4:29

Words are very powerful. God created the world with His words. Your words are creating your world. Use your words to create your marriage, children, health, finances, business and whatever you desire. Speak the promises of God over that situation and let your words be full of grace. Create abundance of whatever you desire with your words. Amen.

*Lord, let the words of my mouth be filled with
edifications and full of grace in Jesus' name.
Amen.*

Day 135
Uncover

"He who covers his sins will not prosper, but whoever confesses and forsake them will have mercy."

Proverbs 28:13

People go through devastating issues in their lives in secret and refuse to get help. Here is a fact: The help you do not ask for you will not receive. God wants to help you prosper. Know today that God already forgave your sins of the past, present and future. Do not live your life in condemnation. Go uncover to our God and ask Him to help you overcome that habitual sin. Amen.

Lord, give me the grace to overcome any habitual sin in my life and give me the grace and wisdom to ask for help in Jesus' name.
Amen.

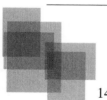

Simple and Powerful Truth to help Jump Start Your Day

Day 136
Fully Convinced

"He did not waver at the promise of God through unbelief, but was strengthened in faith, giving glory to God, and being fully convinced that what He had promised He was also able to perform."

Romans 4:20-21

God does not lie; what He promised in His word He will do.
Be like Abraham, who was fully convinced that God would give Him a child even at an old age. Be fully convinced today that God will heal, deliver, set free, restore, bless, protect, guide, lead, give you wisdom and save. He favors you and will bless you with every promise in His word. Amen.

Lord, give me the grace to be fully convinced concerning Your promises for my life in Jesus' name. Amen.

Day 137
Bear, Forgive and Love

"Bearing with one another, and forgiving one another... But above all these things put on love, which is the bond of perfection."

Colossians 3:13-14

People can hurt you with their words, actions, and inactions. When you experience these actions, do not be mad for long; bear, forgive, and love. For some, the fact you forgive them does not mean you continue to associate with them. You can love from the distance. The key is to not let them control your life. Amen.

Lord, give me the grace to bear, forgive and to love others. Give me the wisdom to proceed with certain relationships in Jesus' name.
Amen.

_____

_____

_____

_____

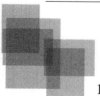

Simple and Powerful Truth to help Jump Start Your Day

Day 138
The Lord's Blessings

"O taste and see that the Lord is good: blessed is the man that trusts in Him."

Psalms 34:8

Do you want to enjoy the blessings of the Lord in every area of your life? If you do, trust in the Lord. Your times of celebration are in sight. Please do not give up; instead step up your level of trust in God, and before you know it your mouth shall be filled with the testimonies of God's goodness. Amen!

Lord, give me the grace to trust in You. I receive
the abundance of Your blessings into my life
in Jesus' name.
Amen.

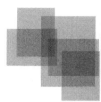

Day 139
Don't Stumble in Words

"We all stumble in many things.
If anyone does not stumble in word,
he is a perfect man, able also to
bridle the whole body."

James 3:2

The power of life and death are in your tongue, your mouth and the words you speak. You can create life or death with what you say. Your word controls your destiny. Do not stumble in words! You might be facing a difficult situation; do not use your words to make it worse. Use words to turn that situation around. Declare the promises of God. Amen.

Lord, give me the grace not to stumble with my
words. Let the words of my mouth be filled with
Your wisdom in Jesus' name.
Amen.

_____

_____

_____

_____

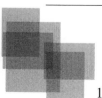

Simple and Powerful Truth to help Jump Start Your Day

Day 140
See Good in Bad

*"And we know that all things
work together for good to those
who love God, to those who are
the called according to
His purpose."*

Romans 8:28

God does not allow bad things to happen to His children, but bad things
can happen to God's children. Just keep on living, and life will keep on
happening. Do not let life happen to you; let life happen for you.
Better yet, make life happen for you. See the positive in your bad situation.
Be more determined and know that God will never fail you in spite of what
happened or is happening in your life. Amen.

*Lord, give me the grace to see Your goodness in
every situation. I thank You that You are working
all things together in my favor in Jesus' name.
Amen.*

_____

_____

_____

_____

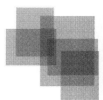

Day 141
The Best Is Yet to Come!

"Eye has not seen, nor ear heard, nor have entered into the heart of man the things which God has prepared for those who love Him."

1 Corinthians 2:9

Do you love God? If you do, be ready for more abundance, goodness, protection, blessings, divine favor, wisdom and so much more. The best is yet to come! Be thankful for what God has done in your life. God has prepared something great for you. Just keep on loving God. The best is yet to come. Amen.

Lord, I thank you for all that You have done, You are doing, and for what You will do in my life. I thank You the best in every area of my life is yet to come in Jesus' name.
Amen.

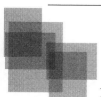

146

Day 142
Yes and Amen Promises

*"For all the promises of God in
him are yea, and in him Amen,
unto the glory of God by us."*

2 Corinthians 1:20

God wants to manifest His promises through you and in you. His promises of peace, protection, wisdom, freedom, health, breakthrough, divine favor and so much more for His glory. He is excited about blessing you; stay in faith, keep standing on and declaring His promises over your life. Live your life daily with the expectation that His yes and amen promises will become reality in your life.

*Lord, give me the grace to consistently believe and
declare Your promises over my life.
I receive Your promises into my life in Jesus' name.
Amen.*

_____

_____

_____

_____

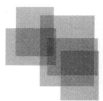

Day 143
Don't Feel Condemned

"There is therefore now no condemnation to those who are in Christ Jesus..."

Romans 8:1

Have you ever felt condemned by a friend, spouse, boss or co-worker?
Have you ever felt condemned because of a sin or a mistake you made?
God does not want you to feel condemned; the Almighty God already
approved you. Do not add any meaning to your mistakes or sins.
Receive the mercy of God and allow Him to live His life through you.
Amen.

*Lord, I thank You that I am not condemned by You,
but approved, loved and accepted by You. Give me
the grace to live my life to honor and the grace to
live the reality of approval by You in Jesus' name.
Amen.*

Simple and Powerful Truth to help Jump Start Your Day

Day 144
Use Your Anger Well!

"Be angry, and do not sin.
Meditate within your heart on
your bed, and be still."

Psalms 4:4

Anger is an emotion that God puts in you. Use your anger to your advantage. Know who your enemy is: the devil. That person or that thing that is causing you to be angry is not your enemy. Get angry at the enemy; rebuke and reject Him over your life and in your relationships. Forgive those who offend and those that did you wrong. Meditate on the goodness of God; this will help subdue the anger. Amen.

Lord, I thank You for Your victory over anger in
my life. Give me the grace to be angry and not
sin in Jesus' name.
Amen.

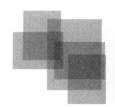

Day 145
Swift and Slow

"So then, my beloved brethren,
let every man be swift to hear,
slow to speak, slow to wrath..."

James 1:19-20

Be swift to listen and to pay attention to your children, spouse, health and relationships and to every area of your life. Be slow to judge, condemn and criticize others. Be swift and slow in your dealings with others and with yourself. It will serve you well. Amen.

Lord, give me the grace to be swift to hear,
slow to speak and slow to anger in all my dealings
in Jesus' name.
Amen.

_____

_____

_____

_____

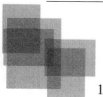

Simple and Powerful Truth to help Jump Start Your Day

Day 146
It's by His Grace

*"For by grace are ye saved
through faith; and that not of
yourselves: it is the gift of God."*

Ephesians 2:8

You are saved by grace through faith; it is a gift from God. Through Jesus Christ, you need to live your life by grace. Your strength, and wisdom are so limited; receive His gift of salvation, health, prosperity and everything that pertains to life and godliness. It is by His grace; receive it into your life for your use. Amen.

*Lord, I receive Your grace to live a victorious
and marvelous life in Jesus' name.
Amen.*

Day 147
Redeemed from Curse

"Christ has redeemed us from the curse of the law, having become a curse for us, for it is written, 'Cursed is everyone who hangs on a tree.'"

Galatians 3:13

You have been redeemed from the curse of sickness, depression, disease, divorce, lack, addiction and anything that is holding you back. See yourself delivered and free. That situation is temporary. You are redeemed of the Lord. Amen.

Lord, I thank You for Your redemption for every area of my life. Give me the grace to enjoy the benefits of Your redemption work in Jesus' name.
Amen.

Simple and Powerful Truth to help Jump Start Your Day

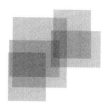

Day 148
Abraham's Blessings

*"That the blessing of Abraham
might come upon the Gentiles
in Christ Jesus, that we might
receive the promise of the
Spirit through faith."*

Galatians 3:14

The redemption through our Lord Jesus Christ gives us access to
Abraham's blessings, the blessing of peace, joy, protection, wisdom,
prosperity and so much more. Abraham's blessings are yours; claim them
by faith. Amen.

*Lord, I thank You for Abraham's blessings and I
thank You for giving me access to these blessings
through Christ Jesus. I receive Your blessings into
my life in Jesus' name.
Amen.*

_____

_____

_____

_____

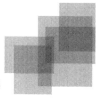

Day 149
God is Faithful!

"Let us hold fast the confession of our hope without wavering, for He who promised is faithful."

Hebrews 10:23

Trust, hope in God with confidence and with great expectation concerning that situation. Our God is a faithful God, He will deliver, set free, provide, give wisdom and protect. What God promised to do in His word, He will provide more than enough in in your life. Have absolute hope in Him, because He is a faithful God. Amen.

Lord, I thank You for You are a faithful God. Give me
the grace to hold fast the confession of my hope in
You without wavering, in Jesus' name.
Amen.

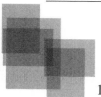

Simple and Powerful Truth to help Jump Start Your Day

Day 150
Faith

"And since we have the same spirit of faith, according to what is written, 'I believed and therefore I spoke,' we also believe and therefore speak."

2 Corinthians 4:13

According to the verse above, faith is believing and speaking. You believe the promise of God concerning that situation, declare, and speak those promises over that situation until you see a desired result. This will keep hope alive in you. Believe and speak the promises over every aspect of your life. Victory is yours! Amen.

Lord, give me the grace to consistently believe and speak Your promises over every area of my life in Jesus' name.
Amen.

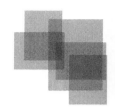

Day 151
Your Actions

"Do not be deceived,
God is not mocked; for whatever a
man sows, that he will also reap."

Galatians 6:7

Every action has corresponding results. There is nothing you can do to
make God love you less, but you will get the result of whatever you sow in
every area of your life. Do not beat yourself up if you feel you have not
been sowing good seeds; the mercy of God can turn things around in your
favor. Get back up and begin again. Amen.

Lord, give me the grace to consistently sow good
seeds in every aspect of my life. I thank You for Your
abundance of blessings in my life in Jesus' name.
Amen.

_____

_____

_____

_____

Simple and Powerful Truth to help Jump Start Your Day

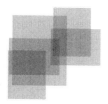

Day 152
Love Above All

*"And above all things have
fervent love for one another,
for love will cover
a multitude of sins."*

1 Peter 4:8

You cannot give what you do not have. If you do not have love, you cannot love others. Love God. Love yourself by receiving the love of God into your life and let love flow from you to others. Love heals and restores. Be love-minded! Amen.

*Lord, give me the grace to be love-minded.
Let Your heavenly love flows into me and through
me to others in Jesus' name.
Amen.*

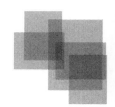

Day 153
Due Season Words

"A man has joy by the answer of his mouth, and a word spoken in due season, how good it is!"

Proverbs 15:23

You words can make or break you and others. Choose your words carefully and speak your words in due season or timely version. Don't talk about important issues when you are angry or tired. Think before you speak. It will serve you well. Amen.

Lord, give me the grace to think before I speak and the grace to speak in due season. Let the words of my mouth be filled with Your wisdom in Jesus' name. Amen.

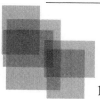

Simple and Powerful Truth to help Jump Start Your Day

Day 154
Trust in Spite of Fear!

*"Whenever I am afraid,
I will trust in You. In God (I will
praise His word), In God I have put
my trust; I will not fear. What can
flesh do to me?"*

Psalms 56:3-4

It is okay to feel fear, but do not allow fear to control your life. Do not focus on your fear; focus on the promises of God. When you are afraid, trust in God and praise Him for His promises concerning that situation. When you do, hope will rise up on the inside of you. Amen.

*Lord, give me the grace to trust in You in the face
of fear. Help me to focus on Your promises instead
of focusing fear, in Jesus' name.
Amen.*

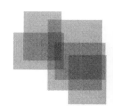

Day 155
The Divine Supplier

"But my God shall supply all your need according to His riches in glory by Christ Jesus."

Philippians 4:19

God will supply all your needs, not according to your bank account, gas prices, your job, or who you know or thought could help you, but according to His riches and glory by our Lord and Savior Jesus Christ. God has an abundance of everything you need. He is your Divine supplier. Amen.

Lord, I thank You that You are my divine supplier
of anything I could ever need. Give me the grace
to trust You, not in my bank account or others,
in Jesus' name.
Amen

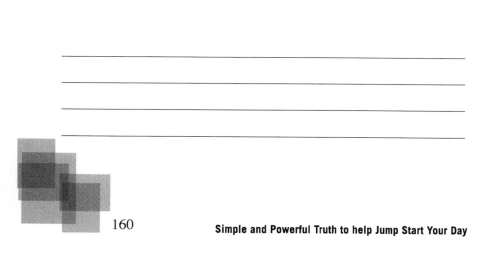

Simple and Powerful Truth to help Jump Start Your Day

Day 156
The Substance

*"Now faith is the substance of
things hoped for, the evidence
of things not seen."*

Hebrews 11:1

If you can see it, you do not need faith for it. Do not believe the negative evidence of the situation. See that situation turning around in your favor through your eyes of faith. Your expectations will become reality through your faith. Expect the goodness of God to overflow your life. Amen.

*Lord, give me the grace to continue to trust and
have faith in You in the face of adversity in Jesus'
name. Amen.*

_____

_____

_____

_____

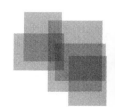

Day 157
By Faith

"But without faith it is impossible
to please Him, for he who comes to
God must believe that He is,
and that He is a rewarder of those
who diligently seek Him."

Hebrews 11:6

The kingdom of God works by faith, not by fear, wants or needs. When you go to God in faith and continually believe and speak His promises over your life, something miraculous happens. God wants to reward your hope and believing with surplus of everything you desire. Amen.

Lord, give me the grace to live by faith and the grace
to diligently seek You at all times in Jesus' name.
Amen.

_____

_____

_____

_____

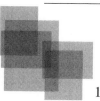

Simple and Powerful Truth to help Jump Start Your Day

Day 158
Instruct, Teach and Guide (I.T.G.)

"I will INSTRUCT you and
TEACH you in the way you should
go;
I will GUIDE you with My eye."

Psalm 32:8

I want you to utilize the INSTRUCT, TEACH, and GUIDE (I.T.G.) method when you are confronted with a situation. God wants to instruct, teach and guide you in all the affaires of your life. Ask Him to instruct, teach and guide you concerning that situation. He promises to never fail or forsake you. Amen.

Lord, give me the grace to follow Your
instructions, teachings and guidance for every
area of my life
in Jesus' name.
Amen.

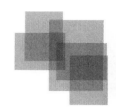

Day 159
God's Word

"So shall My word be that goes forth from My mouth; It shall not return to Me void, But it shall accomplish what I please, And it shall prosper in the thing for which I sent it."

Isaiah 55:11

The word of God has transformation power in it. God has spoken the word of good health, faith, hope, restoration, peace, joy, protection, wisdom, prosperity, and so much more over your life and over any situation you will ever be confronted with. Receive those words by faith into your life today. Amen.

Lord, give me the grace to embrace Your words and
to live by Your words daily in Jesus' name.
Amen.

164

Day 160
The Truth

"And you shall know the truth,
and the truth shall make you
free."

John 8:32

There might be truth to the doctor's report, lacks, debt, depression or setbacks, but there is a greater truth: the Lord's report. His report says that you are free, healed, delivered, prosperous, set free and full of wisdom. Believe the truth of the Lord's report. Amen.

Lord, I thank You for the truth in Your word that
creates freedom. Give me the grace to live by the
truth of Your word in Jesus' name.
Amen.

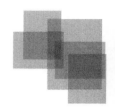

Day 161
Pleasant Words

"Pleasant words are like a honeycomb, sweetness to the soul and health to the bones."

Proverbs 16:24

Your words can create a healthy body, a healthy relationship, healthy children, healthy financial life and healthy emotions. Allow the word of God to dominate your thoughts and declare the words daily to create health in every area of your life. Encourage others with the pleasantness of your words. Amen.

Lord, give me the grace for words of my mouth to be filled with Your wisdom and the grace to encourage others with the pleasantness of my words in Jesus' name.
Amen.

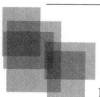

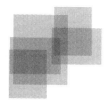

Day 162
No Offense!

"This being so, I myself always strive (discipline my thoughts), to have a conscience without offense toward God and men."

Acts 24:16

Offense is a tactic the enemy uses to frustrate you. It begins with a suggestion, a thought about what a person did or said or what happened to you. Discipline your thoughts by focusing on the goodness of God in your life. No offense! Amen.

Lord, give me the grace over the spirit of offense.
Help me to discipline my thoughts to focus on Your
goodness in Jesus' name.
Amen.

Day 163
Discretion and Understanding

"Discretion will preserve you;
understanding will keep you... "

Proverbs 2:11

Do not jump into a relationship or a decision. Be cautious; it will preserve you. Take some time to reflect, to evaluate your life, on any major or minor business deal decisions. It will give you understanding that will keep you from evil. Amen.

Lord, give me the grace to use discretion in making
major and minor decisions in Jesus' name.
Amen.

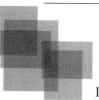

Simple and Powerful Truth to help Jump Start Your Day

Day 164
Goodness of God

"Surely goodness and mercy shall follow me all the days of my life; and I will dwell in the house of the Lord forever."

Psalm 23:6

God wants to be good to you at all times. His goodness and mercy are following you and going before you. Do not focus on that situation or mistake; focus on the goodness of God. Allow the goodness of God to dominate your thoughts and your life. Amen.

Lord, I thank You for Your goodness in my life.
Give me the grace to focus on and dwell on your
goodness daily in Jesus' name.
Amen.

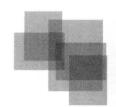

Day 165
Head and Above

*"And the Lord will make you the
head and not the tail; you shall be
above only, and not be beneath..."*

Deuteronomy 28:13

God designed you to be the head, to be above and with the seed of greatness
on the inside of you. That situation is temporary. You are not going under;
you are going over that situation! I declare you will come out unto top, be
the head and above, giving glory to God. Amen.

*Lord, I thank You that I am the head and not the
tail, above only and not beneath. I thank You for the
seed of greatness on the inside of me in Jesus' name.
Amen.*

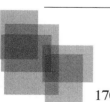

Simple and Powerful Truth to help Jump Start Your Day

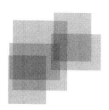

Day 166
Towards

"But each one is tempted when
he is drawn away by his own
desires and enticed."

James 1:14

Your life never remains stagnant. You are constantly moving towards
something. Move your thoughts towards God and His goodness.
Do not move your thoughts towards temptation, depression, frustration and
the circumstance of life. Amen.

Lord, give me the grace to move my thoughts
towards Your righteousness, goodness, wisdom
and peace in Jesus' name.
Amen.

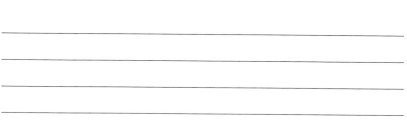

Day 167
Service

"With goodwill doing service,
as to the Lord, and not to men."

Ephesians 6:7

The best service is the service to self. Praying, giving, forgiving, dwelling on the goodness of God and loving will serve you well. Servicing others begins first by servicing yourself, which is taking time to become the best so that you can give your best. Amen.

Lord, give me grace to be the best I can be and
so that I can give the best to the people in my life.
Give me the grace to serve You and others with
goodwill in Jesus' name.
Amen.

Simple and Powerful Truth to help Jump Start Your Day

Day 168
A-Plus Life

*"As His divine power has given
to us all things that pertain
to life and godliness."*

2 Peter 1:3

God wants you to have an A-plus life. You need to take hold of everything
God has given to you to enjoy. Believe and trust that everything that
pertains to life and godliness will become reality in your life. Live your life
by faith and not by fear. You are made for more than enough. Amen.

*Lord, I receive everything that pertains to life and
godliness in every area of my life. Nothing will
hold me back in Jesus' name.
Amen.*

Day 169
Good and Perfect Gift

"Every good gift and every perfect
gift is from above, and comes down
from the Father of lights, with
whom there is no variation
or shadow of turning."

James 1:17

God delights in you, He wants to give you good and perfect gifts for every area of your life. He wants to give you exactly what you need to make your life better. Trust Him for the good and perfect gift concerning that situation. Amen.

Lord, I thank You for Your good and perfect gifts.
I receive them for every area of my life
in Jesus' name.
Amen.

Simple and Powerful Truth to help Jump Start Your Day

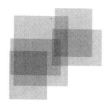

Day 170
Living Life

*"I (Jesus Christ) have come that
you might have LIFE
and have it more abundantly..."*

John 10:10

You are not designed to barely get by; you are designed to live an abundant life. God wants you to live your life to the fullest; He wants you to break free from anything that is holding you back. I declare that you will live the abundant life of God. Amen.

*Lord, give me the grace to live my life to honor
You. I thank You for the abundant life You came to
give me. I receive Your grace to live abundantly,
serving and honoring you in Jesus' name.
Amen.*

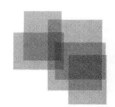

Day 171
Integrity Living

"The integrity of the upright will guide them, but the perversity of the unfaithful will destroy them."

Proverbs 11:3

Integrity is honoring your word; it is a way of being. It is not making yourself and others wrong; it allows you to be powerful in your relationships and in your conversations, and it gives you peace. Living with integrity allows you to guide your life. Amen.

*Lord, give me the grace to live a life of integrity in
all my dealings, in Jesus' name.
Amen.*

Simple and Powerful Truth to help Jump Start Your Day

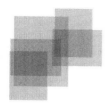

Day 172
Forces of Life

"Keep your heart with all diligence, for out of it spring the issues (forces) of life."

Proverbs 4:23

There is a life-producing force on the inside of you. This force responds to whatever you feed it – either negative or positive – and produces accordingly. Feed your mind with the promises of God, and it will produce life accordingly. Amen.

Lord, give me the grace to keep my heart with all diligence. Give me the grace to feed my mind with Your promises in Jesus' name.
Amen.

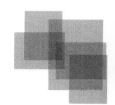

Day 173
Examined Life

*"Examine yourselves as to
whether you are in the faith.
Test yourselves..."*

2 Corinthians 13:5

Socrates, said, "An unexamined life is a life that is not worth living."
How are you? This is a question you need to consistently ask yourself as
it relates to every aspect of your life. Take inventory of your life and make
necessary adjustments. Amen.

*Lord, give me the grace to consistently examine
every aspect of my life in Jesus' name.
Amen.*

_____

_____

_____

_____

Simple and Powerful Truth to help Jump Start Your Day

Day 174
Delight Yourself

*"Delight yourself also in the Lord,
and He shall give you the desires
of your heart."*

Psalms 37:4

When you delight yourself in the Lord by reading His word, through prayer of faith, praises and worship, fellowshipping with others believers, living your life to honor God and giving, God will give you the desires of your heart. Delight yourself in Him today. Amen.

*Lord, give me the grace to delight myself in You
at all times in Jesus' name.
Amen.*

_____

_____

_____

_____

Day 175
Ask, Believe and Receive!

"Therefore I say to you, whatever
things you ask when you pray,
believe that you receive them,
and you will have them."

Mark 11:24

Every achievement begins with a desire. Ask what you desire through faith in prayer and also immediately believe that you receive what you desire and live your life daily with great expectation. Give thanks, for your desire is coming into your life. Ask, believe, and receive, because your best is yet to come. Amen.

Lord, give me the grace to ask in faith, believe in
faith and to receive in faith in Jesus' name.
Amen.

_____

_____

_____

_____

Simple and Powerful Truth to help Jump Start Your Day

Day 176
Praise God!

"But thou art holy,
O thou that inhabits the
praises of Israel."

Psalms 22:3 (KJV)

God inhabits (lives and dwells) in your praises. Praises connects you easily to God, give you inspirations, revelations, dreams and visions and creates deliverance from evil. Praise Him in the storm and praise Him in good times. Praise God, for He is good and does good. Praise produces more of the goodness of God in your life. Amen.

Lord, give me the grace to consistently praise You.
Fill my mouth with praises of Your goodness in
Jesus' name.
Amen.

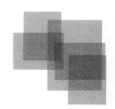

Day 177
Fellowshipping

*"Not forsaking the assembling of
ourselves together, as is the manner
of some, but exhorting one another,
and so much the more as you see
the Day approaching."*

Hebrews 10:25

God delights in your fellowship with other believers. Go to a
Bible-believing, faith-filled, loving church. Attend a church that will lift
you up, inspire, love and encourage you to be your best and get involved.
If you want to grow, go to church. Amen.

*Lord, give me the grace to find a church that makes
everything about Your grace and attend that church
faithfully in Jesus' name.
Amen.*

Simple and Powerful Truth to help Jump Start Your Day

Day 178
Righteous Living!

"If we say that we have no sin,
we deceive ourselves,
and the truth is not in us.
If we confess our sins,
He is faithful and just to forgive
us our sins and to cleanse us
from all unrighteousness."

1 John 1:8-9

Living a righteous life is simply living your life to honor God. It is not about perfection, about not sinning; it is about having a desire to please God. God is not surprised about your shortcomings. Get back up and receive the mercy of God. Amen.

Lord, give me the grace to run to You when I fall.
Give me the grace to live my life to honor
in Jesus' name. Amen.

_____

_____

_____

_____

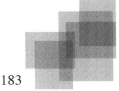

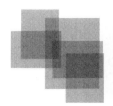

Day 179
Enjoy Giving

"Give, and it will be given to you:
good measure, pressed down,
shaken together, and running
over will be put into your bosom.
For with the same measure
that you use, it will be measured
back to you."

Luke 6:38

Giving is an honor and a privilege. How do you see money and your resources? What is your relationship with money? Do not allow giving to be a burden to you; enjoy giving. When you give you have more. Give more of what you desire. Your giving is the seed that creates your future harvest. Amen.

Lord, give me the grace to give my time, money and
resources with a joyful heart in Jesus' name.
Amen.

_____

_____

_____

_____

184

Day 180
Giving Grace

*"Through the Lord's mercies
(Grace) we are not consumed,
because His compassions fail not.
They are new every morning;
great is Your faithfulness."*

Lamentations 3:22-23

Grace is undeserved, unearned favor of God in your life. God has given you all the grace you will ever need. Now give that grace to others, God wants to channel His grace through you to others. Allow His grace to flow through you to others, and His giving grace will cause you to overcome. Amen.

*Lord, I receive Your grace for every area of my
life. Let Your grace flow through me to others
in Jesus' name.
Amen.*

_____

_____

_____

_____

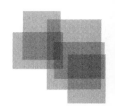

Day 181
Receiving Grace

"And He said to me,
'My grace is sufficient for you,
for My strength is made perfect in
weakness.' Therefore most gladly
I will rather boast in my infirmities,
that the power of Christ may rest
upon me."

2 Corinthians 12:9

His grace is sufficient for that situation confronting you. His grace is reproducing in your life daily. Receive His grace for your daily use today. God will not force His grace on you. Actively position yourself daily to consistently receive His free grace. Amen.

Lord, I thank You that Your grace is sufficient for any situation
confronting me. Give me the grace to consistently rely on and
tap into Your grace daily in Jesus' name.
Amen.

_____

_____

_____

_____

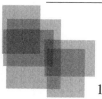

Simple and Powerful Truth to help Jump Start Your Day

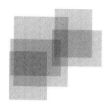

Day 182
Accountable Grace

"What shall we say then?
Shall we continue in sin, that
GRACE may abound
(thrive, flourish, prosper, overflow,
be plentiful and be abundant)?"

Romans 6:1

You have to be accountable for what you watch, what you say, what you do, what you listen to and whom you associate yourself with. Grace does not demand accountability but requests accountability. Do you have a sin you can't overcome? Allow the grace of God to cause you to overcome. Amen.

Lord, give me the grace to be accountable to
You and others in all my dealings in Jesus' name.
Amen.

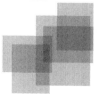

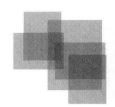

Day 183
Consistent Grace

"Let us therefore come boldly to the throne of grace, that we may obtain mercy and find grace to help in time of need."

Hebrews 4:16

Be consistent in giving grace, in receiving grace and in being accountable to grace. To fully enjoy the grace of God, you have to be consistent in dwelling on the grace of God. Go boldly to His throne of grace daily. Amen.

Lord, give me the grace to go boldly to Your throne of grace daily. Give me the grace to receive Your grace, to give Your grace and to be consistent in being accountable to Your grace in Jesus' name. Amen.

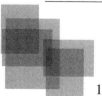

Simple and Powerful Truth to help Jump Start Your Day

Day 184
Excelling Grace

"But grow in the grace and knowledge of our Lord and Savior Jesus Christ. To Him be the glory both now and forever. Amen."

2 Peter 3:18

When you learn to give and receive grace, you become accountable to grace. When you constantly give, receive; you have no choice, but to excel in grace. You can truly say, "His grace is sufficient for me." Amen.

Lord, give me the grace to grow from grace to grace. I declare, I will excel in Your grace in every area of my life in Jesus' name.
Amen.

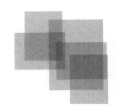

Day 185
Love is Patient

"Love is patient..."

1 Corinthians 13:4 (NIV)

Do not beat yourself; be patient with yourself and with others. God is not mad at you; He loves you and He wants you to love others and yourself. Do not expect others and yourself to change overnight. Exercise some patience and love unconditionally. Love is patient! Amen.

Lord, give me the grace to be patient in love with
others and myself in Jesus' name.
Amen.

_____

_____

_____

_____

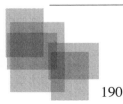

Simple and Powerful Truth to help Jump Start Your Day

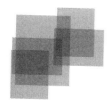

Day 186
Show Kindness

*"For His merciful kindness is
great (countless, unlimited,
and abundant) toward us..."*

Psalms 117:2

Love is kind, caring, nice, sympathetic, generous, gentle, thoughtful,
compassionate and benevolent. Receive the loving-kindness of God into
your life and allow it to flow from you to others. Be kind to someone today.
Amen.

*Lord, give me the grace to consistently show
kindness to others. I receive Your merciful
kindness into my life in Jesus' name.
Amen.*

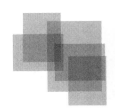

Day 187
No Envy

"Love...does not envy."

1 Corinthians 13:4 (NIV)

Have you ever met a person who is full of jealousy and greed? They drive you crazy? Jealousy creates selfish ambition and confusion. Make sure you have no envy in you and separate or limit yourself from people that are jealous. It will serve you well. Amen.

Lord, reveal any envy in me and give me the grace
to overcome envy in my life. Give me the grace
and the wisdom to overcome people with envy in
Jesus' name.
Amen.

_____

_____

_____

_____

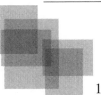

Simple and Powerful Truth to help Jump Start Your Day

Day 188
Boast in the Lord!

"Love... does not boast
and Love is not proud..."

1 Corinthians 13:4

Loving God, loving yourself and others is what life is all about.
Love does not boast; pride and boasting destroys. If you need to boast,
boast about the goodness of God in your life. The more you praise Him,
the more His blessings will overflow your life. Amen.

Lord, reveal any form of boasting in my life and
give me the grace to overcome. Give me the grace
to boast Your goodness in my life, in Jesus' name.
Amen.

_____

_____

_____

_____

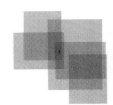

Day 189
Honor

"Love...
does not dishonor others..."

1 Corinthian 13:5 (NIV)

Anytime you dishonor, you do not love. You love the people in your life by honoring them. Honor God by the way you live your life daily and let that honor flow through you to others. Honor gives encouragement to others and blessings to you. Amen.

Lord, give me the grace to live my life to honor
You and others. Reveal any element of dishonor
in my life and give me the grace to overcome
in Jesus' name.
Amen.

_____

_____

_____

_____

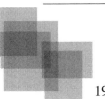

Simple and Powerful Truth to help Jump Start Your Day

Day 190
Self Seeking

"Love…is not self-seeking…"

1 Corinthians 13:5 (NIV)

If you do not love yourself, how can you expect to love others and how can you expect others to love you? Love is not self-seeking; one of the best ways to avoid self-seeking is taking care of yourself, so that you can give your best to others. Amen.

> *Lord, give me the grace to be the best I can be so*
> *that I can give my best to others in Jesus' name.*
> *Amen.*

Day 191
Not Easily Angered

"Love…
is not easily angered…"

1 Corinthians 13:5 (NIV)

Be angry but do not allow your anger to control you. Do not be easily angered; give people breaks. Do not allow issues to accumulate. Address and confront issues with love, on time and at the right time. Be wise in your choice of what you get angry about. Amen.

Lord, give me the grace to allow my anger to be
mixed with Your wisdom in Jesus' name.
Amen.

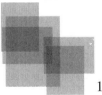

Simple and Powerful Truth to help Jump Start Your Day

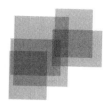

Day 192
Keep Records

"Love...
keeps no record of wrongs."

1 Corinthian 13:5 (NIV)

God does not keep the record of your wrongdoings and you shouldn't keep the record of the wrongdoings of others in your conscious and sub-conscious mind. Instead, keep the record of the goodness of God in your life and the good things in others. Love, but be wise in your relationships. Amen.

Lord, give me the grace to keep the records of Your
goodness in my life and record of good things in
others in Jesus' name.
Amen.

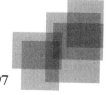

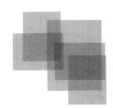

Day 193
Red Flags

*"Love does not delight in evil
but rejoices with the truth"*

1 Corinthians 13:6 (NIV)

It is amazing how people live their lives sweeping stuff under the carpet.
Do not ignore the red flags in your life and in your relationships.
The best way to love others and yourself is to address the red flags in love.
What you address on time will save you many years of trouble. Amen.

*Lord, give me the grace to pay attention to minor
and major details in life and in my relationships
in Jesus' name.
Amen.*

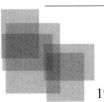

Simple and Powerful Truth to help Jump Start Your Day

Day 194
Love Always Protects

"Love...always protects..."

1 Corinthians 13:7

Love always protects, defends, guards, keeps, shields, shelters and safeguards. Whatever you do not protect you will eventually lose. Protect your marriage, children, finances, health, relationships and heart. Love always protects. Amen.

Lord, give me the grace to protect the people in my
life and Your blessings in my life in Jesus' name.
Amen.

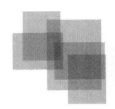

Day 195
Love Always Trusts

"...Love...always trusts..."

1 Corinthians 13:7

When you stop trusting you stop loving. You might not trust a person's character, but trust the person, believe the best of them. You might not do business with them, because of their character; trust that God will transform that person. Remember, you do not have to be close to them, but you can love them from a distance. God is love, and we have His love in us. Love always trusts! Amen.

Lord, give me the grace and the wisdom to always
love and trust in Jesus' name.
Amen.

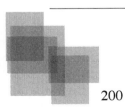

200   **Simple and Powerful Truth to help Jump Start Your Day**

Day 196
Love Always Hopes

"...Love always hopes..."

1 Corinthians 13:7 (NIV)

Love always has positive expectations regardless of what is going on. Have positive expectation about that situation and about that relationship. When you hope in God and have hope in others you are showing love. Amen.

Lord, give me the grace to always love in hope
in Jesus' name.
Amen.

Day 197
Love Always Perseveres

"...Love always perseveres..."

1 Corinthians 13:7

Love always preservers with patience, kindness, truth, honor, trust, protection and hope, but love does not envy, boast or engage in self-seeking. Love is not easily angered and does not keep records of wrongs. When you do not give up on God and on others, you are showing love. Amen.

*Lord, give me the grace to persevere in love
in Jesus' name.
Amen.*

_____
_____
_____
_____

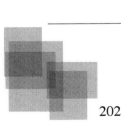

Simple and Powerful Truth to help Jump Start Your Day

Day 198
Press Forward!

"I press toward the goal for the prize of the upward call of God in Christ Jesus."

Philippians 3:14

If you keep living, life will keep happening. You will be disappointed, hurt or talked about, you might fall or sin and you might experience losses. Do not give up on hope. Press forward and allow the grace of God to flow into your life, and it will cause you to rise again. Keep pressing forward. Amen.

Lord, give me the grace to keep pressing forward in Your goodness and do not allow me to give up in difficult situations. Help me to keep trusting in Your goodness in Jesus' name.
Amen.

_____

_____

_____

_____

Day 199
Please God!

"And whatever you do,
do it heartily, as to the Lord and
not to men, knowing that from the
Lord you will receive the reward of
the inheritance; for you serve the
Lord Christ."

Colossians 3:23-24

One of the easiest ways to fail in life is to live your life to please others.
You are not called to please people; you are called to love people.
Do not allow pressure from people to cause you to please them.
Do everything wholeheartedly to please God. Amen.

Lord, give me the grace to love You and others.
Give me the grace to please You in all my dealings
in Jesus' name.
Amen.

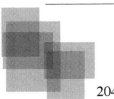

204

Day 200
Family First!

*"And He stretched out His hand
toward His disciples and said,
"Here are my mother and My
brothers! For whoever does the
will of My Father in heaven
is My brother and sister
and mother."*

Matthew 12:49-50

Put God first, then family that inspires you to be the best, speaks life into you and inspires you to live your life to honor God. Your first family is the one that will set you apart for success in every area of your life. Amen.

*Lord, give me the grace to put You first,
the grace to serve and the grace to love my family
unconditionally in Jesus' name.
Amen.*

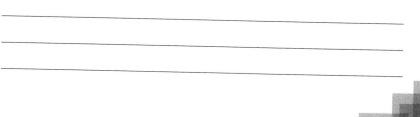

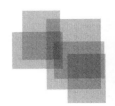

Day 201
Pay Attention!

*"Examine yourselves as to
whether you are in the faith.
Test yourselves..."*

2 Corinthians 13:5

Constantly, evaluate your life and your associations and make adjustments accordingly. The time spent examining every aspect of your life is the most valuable time. Do not live a life of neglect; pay attention to the affairs of your life. Amen.

*Lord, give me the grace and the wisdom to
consistently examine my life, along with dealings,
in Jesus' name.
Amen*

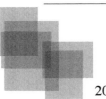

Simple and Powerful Truth to help Jump Start Your Day

Day 202
Acknowledge Him!

"In all your ways
acknowledge Him,
and He shall direct your paths. "

Proverbs 3:6

God wants to help you concerning that situation confronting you. Acknowledge Him today. He will give you wisdom, favor, divine connection and comfort, and He will direct your path leading you to the path of success. Amen.

Lord, instead of worrying give me the grace
to acknowledge You consistently in my life
in Jesus' name.
Amen.

_____

_____

_____

_____

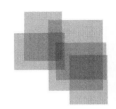

Day 203
Love In Spite Of

"Judge not, and you shall not be
judged. Condemn not, and you
shall not be condemned.
Forgive, and you will be forgiven."

Luke 6:37

You will have reasons to judge and condemn and difficulty forgiving others
and yourself. Love them in spite of what they did or said about you.
You can love others from a distance; do not allow the stupidity of others to
cause you to fall. Amen.

Lord, give me the grace to love in spite of the wrongs
others did to me. Give me the grace to not judge and
condemn others, in Jesus' name.
Amen.

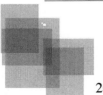

Simple and Powerful Truth to help Jump Start Your Day

Day 204
Cast your Burden!

"Cast your burden on the Lord,
and He shall sustain you;
He shall never permit the
righteous to be moved."

Psalm 55:22

God wants to help and sustain you through that situation. He does not want you to fail and barely get by in life. He wants you to cast that situation to Him and to trust in Him to see you through to success. Keep doing your best and cast that burden to Him today. You are not going under. Amen.

Lord, give me the grace to cast my burdens to You.
I thank You for Your victory in my life
in Jesus' name.
Amen.

_____

_____

_____

_____

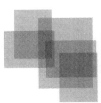

Day 205
Use Your Disappointments

"In everything give thanks;
for this is the will of God
in Christ Jesus for you."

1 Thessalonians 5:18

Use your disappointments; do not allow your disappointment to use you.
Do not waste your disappointments; use them to your advantage.
Savor the life out of each disappointment. This is not the time to complain
or get discouraged; it is the time to arise and get going. Give thanks not for
disappointments but for the fact that God is with you. He will always cause
you to triumph. Amen.

Lord, give me the grace to give You thanks in the
midst of a difficult situation, not for the situation, but
for my victory in Jesus' name.
Amen.

_____

_____

_____

_____

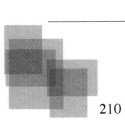

Simple and Powerful Truth to help Jump Start Your Day

Day 206
New Things Happening

"Do not remember the former things, nor consider the things of old.
Behold, I will do a new thing..."

Isaiah 43:18-19

Have the pressures of life left you wounded, broken and disappointed? Maybe you are experiencing some level of success right now? God is about to do new things in your life that will propel you to a new level. In fact, new things are happening right now in your life. Arise and go. Amen.

Lord, I thank You for the new things You are doing in my life. Give me the grace to grasp hold of Your new things in every area of my life in Jesus' name.
Amen.

_____

_____

_____

_____

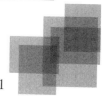

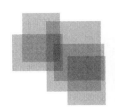

Day 207
Help Selflessly

*"Be hospitable to one another
without grumbling."*

1 Peter 4:9

When you make everything about God, God will make everything about you. When you make everything about others, they might not make everything about you. but if you continue to be hospitable, God will be your vindicator, He will reward you abundantly. Amen.

*Lord, give me the grace to be hospitable consistently
without grumbling in Jesus' name.
Amen.*

_____

_____

_____

_____

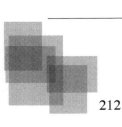

Simple and Powerful Truth to help Jump Start Your Day

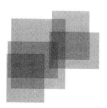

Day 208
The Good Lord

"The Lord is good, a stronghold
in the day of trouble; And He
knows (recognizes, has knowledge
of,
and understands) those who
trust in Him."

Nahum 1:7

The Lord is good and He knows about the situation confronting you. My friend, He is the way, your restorer in trouble times. He wants you to trust in Him for your restoration and your breakthrough. Trust the Good Lord today. Amen.

Lord, I trust in You and in Your goodness.
Give me the grace to continue to trust in You in
difficult times in Jesus' name.
Amen.

_____

_____

_____

_____

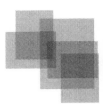

Day 209
Don't Complain – Confront!

"Let all bitterness, wrath, anger,
clamor, and evil speaking be put
away from you, with all malice.
And be kind to one another,
tenderhearted, forgiving one
another, even as God in Christ
forgave you."

Ephesians 4:31-32

The enemy wants you to complain, criticize, judge and condemn.
You cannot change what you complained about, but you can change what
you are willing to confront. Be kind and compassionate and confront the
situation in love. Amen.

Lord, instead of complaining, give me the grace to
confront others or the situation, in love, through You
in Jesus' name.
Amen.

_____

_____

_____

_____

Day 210
Over Limitations

*"Now thanks be to God
who always leads us in
triumph in Christ."*

2 Corinthians 2:14

Society, environment, family, friends and you can set limitations in your life, but the worst limitation is the one you set for yourself. You cannot be limited by a situation and by others without your consent. You are designed to live a triumphant life. Make up your mind that you are over any form of limitations in every aspect of your life. Amen.

*I declare that every limitation that is set over
your life is destroyed, and God is causing you to
triumph in Christ in Jesus' name.
Amen.*

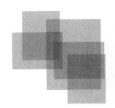

Day 211
Through Christ

"I can do all this through
him who gives me strength."

Philippians 4:13

Whatever it is that is holding you back from living a happy, healthy and prosperous life is a limitation, but through Christ you can overcome by His strength working in and through you. Don't accept any limitation as your lot in life. Amen.

I declare that you overcome every limitation in your
life through Christ who infuses strength into you
in Jesus' name.
Amen.

_____

_____

_____

_____

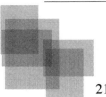

Simple and Powerful Truth to help Jump Start Your Day

Day 212
He's Not Resting!

*"Be sober, be vigilant;
because your adversary the devil
walks about like a roaring lion,
seeking whom he may devour."*

1 Peter 5:8

The enemy is not resting concerning you, but God is not resting concerning you either. The One in the inside of you is greater than the enemy in the world. Be sober and vigilant with your praises, prayers and the word of God. Victory is yours! Amen.

*Lord, give me the grace to be sober and be vigilant
in every area of my life in Jesus' name.
Amen.*

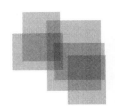

Day 213
Uniquely Made

"I will praise You, for I am
fearfully and wonderfully made..."

Psalms 139:14

God uniquely made you. You are full of talents and creative abilities.
You might have barriers, but nothing is wrong with who you are.
Whatever barrier is holding you back is temporary; you are one of a kind.
Do not ever think less of yourself; you are valuable, you have it in you to
win and you have the seed of greatness in the inside of you. Amen.

Lord, I thank You for depositing Your greatness into
me. Give me the grace to optimize the greatness
inside of me in Jesus' name.
Amen.

_____

_____

_____

_____

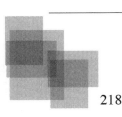

Simple and Powerful Truth to help Jump Start Your Day

Day 214
Walk of Integrity

"He who walks with integrity walks securely, but he who perverts his ways will become known."

Proverbs 10:9

When you walk in integrity you have peace, joy, harmony, tranquility and favor. Integrity gives you freedom and boldness to make wise decisions. Integrity is honesty with God, others and yourself. It gives you confidence. Walk in integrity. Amen.

Lord, give me the grace to walk in integrity in all circumstances in Jesus name.
Amen.

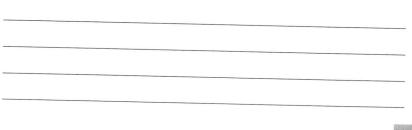

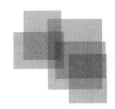

Day 215
God Will Help You

"For I, the Lord your God, will
hold your right hand, saying to
you, 'Fear not, I will help you.'"

Isaiah 41:13

You will overcome that situation that is confronting you, because God says He will help you. Commit that situation to God right now and trust Him to help you. Let hope rise up on the inside of you. God is telling you not to fear and that He will help you to overcome. Amen.

Lord, give me the grace to trust that You will help
me. I thank You for holding my right hand, for Your
victory over fear and for Your help in Jesus' name.
Amen.

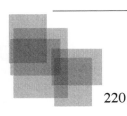

Simple and Powerful Truth to help Jump Start Your Day

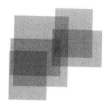

Day 216
Watch Out Now!

"Can a man take fire to his bosom, and his clothes not be burned?
Can one walk on hot coals, and his feet not be seared?"

Proverbs 6:27-28

Watch out now! Watch your relationships, not everyone, including your extended family members, immediate family and your best friends, are right for you. You cannot play with fire and not get burned. What you do not protect you will eventually lose. Amen.

Lord, give me the grace to pay attention to every detail of my life. Give me the grace to walk in Your wisdom in Jesus' name.
Amen.

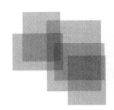

Day 217
Be Transformed

"And do not be conformed to this world, but be transformed by the renewing of your mind, that you may prove what is that good and acceptable and perfect will of God."

Romans 12:2

You can be conformed to the patterns of this world without you doing anything. You can transform any area of your life, overcome a situation by renewing your mind and conform to the promises of God for every area of your life. Feed your mind with the promises of God. Amen.

Lord, give me the grace to feed my mind with
Your promises daily in Jesus' name.
Amen.

_____

_____

_____

_____

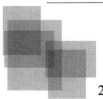

Simple and Powerful Truth to help Jump Start Your Day

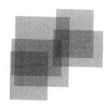

Day 218
Fear No Evil

"Yea, though I walk through the valley of the shadow of death, I will fear no evil; For You are with me; Your rod and Your staff, they comfort me."

Psalms 23:4

Are you overwhelmed with a situation confronting you and as a result are filled with fear? I want to encourage you to fear no evil. God is with you, fighting your battles for you and comforting you. See God in that situation causing you to triumph. Fear no evil. Amen.

Lord, I thank You for victory over fear. I thank You for Your comfort and for causing me to triumph in Jesus' name.
Amen

_____

_____

_____

_____

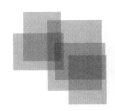

Day 219
Watch Your Actions

"Can a man take fire to his bosom,
and his clothes not be burned?
Can one walk on hot coals,
and his feet not be seared?"

Proverbs 6:27-28

Watch your actions! Are your actions in line with the word of God?
Your actions are either progressing you or regressing you. You cannot walk
on hot coals and not have your feet burned. Do your best to develop the
characters of God in your life daily. Amen.

Lord, give me the grace to develop godly characters
in all my dealings in Jesus' name.
Amen.

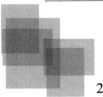

Simple and Powerful Truth to help Jump Start Your Day

Day 220
God Is Fighting for You

" For the Lord your God is
He who goes with you,
to fight for you against your
enemies, to save you!'"

Deuteronomy 20:4

Have you tried and failed several times to overcome a situation? God is going to fight for you against the enemies of fear, depression, addictions, pains, lacks, sickness and disease. Ask God today to fight for you, and He will give you the victory. Trust Him for your victory today. Amen.

Lord, I thank You for fighting my battles for me.
I thank You for Your victory in my life
in Jesus' name.
Amen.

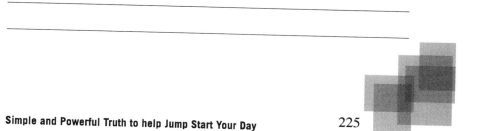

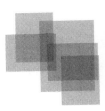

Day 221
You Have the Victory!

"And the Lord said to Joshua,
'Do not fear them, for I have
delivered them into your hand;
not a man of them shall
stand before you.'"

Joshua 10:8

My friend, God already gave you the victory over that situation.
See yourself victorious; see yourself overcoming that situation.
Do not fear the situation confronting you. God already gave you the victory,
favor and divine connections. Believe and receive it. Amen.

Lord, I thank You for Your victory in every area of
my life. I receive your favor and divine connections
into my life. I thank You that no weapon formed
against me shall prosper in Jesus' name.
Amen.

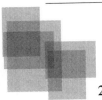

Simple and Powerful Truth to help Jump Start Your Day

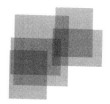

Day 222
Be Steadfast

"Therefore, my beloved brethren, be steadfast, immovable, always abounding in the work of the Lord, knowing that your labor is not in vain in the Lord."

1 Corinthians 15:58

What you do consistently will eventually become part who you are. Consistently do the right things, declaring the promises of God over your life and associating with the right people. Be steadfast in love, hope, faith and righteousness. Amen.

Lord, give me the grace to be steadfast and immovable in my relationships with You and in all my dealings in Jesus' name.
Amen.

_____

_____

_____

_____

Day 223
Your Hope and Trust

"For You are my hope,
O Lord GOD;
You are my trust from my youth."

Psalm 71:5

God is your hope and trust. He wants you to put your hope and trust in Him all day long. When you do, He will fill your heart with peace that surpasses all understanding. I declare peace, joy, harmony, tranquility and favor over your life. Amen.

Lord, I thank You that You are my hope and trust.
Give me the grace to put my hope and trust in You
in Jesus' name.
Amen.

_____

_____

_____

_____

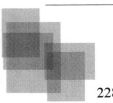

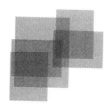

Day 224
Thanks and Victory!

"But thanks be to God,
who gives us the victory through
our Lord Jesus Christ."

1 Corinthians 15:57

When you give thanks you have victory. Give thanks over that situation, not for the situation. Give thanks, because God already won the victory for you. In the midst of that situation, look for something to give thanks for. Victory is yours! Amen.

Lord, give me the grace to give You thanks at
all times. Fill my mouth with Your praise
in Jesus' name.
Amen.

_____

_____

_____

_____

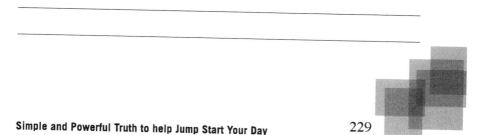

Day 225
Don't Give Up!

*"I have fought the good fight,
I have finished the race,
I have kept the faith."*

2 Timothy 4:7

The enemy will do anything to cause you to give up, because he knows that you are closer to your breakthroughs. No matter how difficult things seem, how many times you have tried and failed, no matter who believes or who doesn't believe in you, do not give up. Keep on hoping, believing and trusting in God. Your victory is in sight. Amen.

*Lord, give me the grace not give up in the face of
adversity and give me the grace to fight the good
fight. I declare Your victory over my life
in Jesus' name.
Amen.*

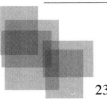

Simple and Powerful Truth to help Jump Start Your Day

Day 226
At Just the Right Time

"So let's not get tired of doing what is good. At just the right time we will reap a harvest of blessing if we don't give up."

Galatians 6:9 (NLT)

You will reap a harvest of blessings at just the right time, when you refuse to give up on doing what is good in the face of difficulty, when you keep on believing and when you become a prisoner of positive expectations. Harvests of blessings will overflow in your life. Amen.

Lord, give me the grace to not get tired of doing what is good in all my dealings. I thank You for Your harvest of blessings in every area of my life in Jesus' name.
Amen.

_____

_____

_____

_____

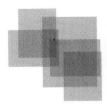

Day 227
Doing the Mundane Well

"And whatever you do in word or deed, do all in the name of the Lord Jesus, giving thanks to God the Father through Him."

Colossians 3:17

Little is much with God in it, and you don't need to do a lot to be successful. You just need to love a little, speak faith, hope, give and take little actions well daily in the name of Jesus, and before you know it you are free, delivered, prosperous and full of health serving the Lord with joy and gladness. Amen.

Lord, give me the grace to do the little things well.
Let my words and actions reflect Your glory to others
in Jesus' name.
Amen.

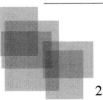

Day 228
Eliminate your Anxiety

"When wisdom enters your heart,
and knowledge is pleasant to your
soul, discretion will preserve you;
Understanding will keep you."

Proverbs 2:10-11

Do you have an anxiety? If you do, you can reduce or eliminate the anxiety through wisdom, knowledge, discretion and understanding. Instead of worrying, ask God for wisdom and guidance and declare His favor over that situation. Amen.

Lord, give me the grace to consistently seek Your
wisdom in all my dealings in Jesus' name.
Amen.

_____

_____

_____

_____

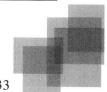

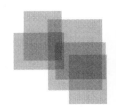

Day 229
A Joyful Heart!

*"A merry heart (joyful heart)
does good, like medicine..."*

Proverbs 17:22

The enemy is after your joy, because joy is good medicine for the situation confronting you. You cannot keep a joyful person down, and do not allow that situation to steal your joy. You are not joyful, because of the situation, but you are joyful because God is on your side, fighting your battles for you. Amen.

*Lord, give me the grace to have a joyful heart all
times in Jesus' name.
Amen.*

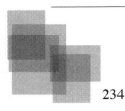

Day 230
Alert and Sober

*"Be sober, be vigilant; because
your adversary the devil walks
about like a roaring lion,
seeking whom he may devour."*

1 Peter 5:8

The enemy is the master of distractions. He will distract you from the promises of God and from what is important to you. The enemy is defeated over your life. What you do not pay attention to you will eventually lose. Pay attention and praise your way to victory. Amen.

*Lord, open my eyes to all the tactics of the enemy
in all my dealings. Give me the grace to be sober
and vigilant and take positive, appropriate action
against the enemy in Jesus' name.
Amen.*

Day 231
The Thief

"The thief does not come except to steal, and to kill, and to destroy. I have come that they may have life, and that they may have it more abundantly."

John 10:10

The enemy's goal is to steal, kill and destroy what makes your life better. He uses the patterns in your life to accomplish this. Observe the patterns in your life; you will be amazed what needs improvement and what or who needs to be eliminated. Amen.

Lord, I thank You for Your restoration in every area of my life. I thank You for Your abundant life in my life in Jesus' name.
Amen.

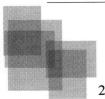

Simple and Powerful Truth to help Jump Start Your Day

Day 232
The Greater One

"You, dear children, are from God and have overcome them, because the one who is in you is greater than the one who is in the world."

1 John 4:4

The patterns you have developed in different areas of your life control and mold your life. They control your behavior, personality and thought processes. The greater one lives on the inside of you; allow Him through His word to transform the patterns in your life for your benefits. Amen.

Lord, I thank You that You are greater than any negative patterns in my life and anything confronting me. I thank You that I am victorious in Jesus' name. Amen.

_____

_____

_____

_____

Day 233
Give Thanks!

"Let us come before His presence with thanksgiving; Let us shout joyfully to Him with psalms."

Psalms 95:2

Instead of focusing on your setbacks and on what did not work out, focus on giving thanks. Enter today with thanksgiving in your heart, not only with the list of your wants. When you give thanks you have clarity and inspirations. The goodness of God will abound in your life today. Amen.

Lord, give me the grace to enter each day with thanksgiving. I Praise You for who You are and for Your goodness in my life in Jesus' name.
Amen.

_____

_____

_____

_____

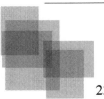

Simple and Powerful Truth to help Jump Start Your Day

Day 234
He's Your Portion

" 'The Lord is my portion,' says my soul, 'Therefore I hope in Him!' "

Lamentations 3:24

The Lord is your portion of peace, favor, abundance, health and wisdom in every area of your life. He wants to give you a large portion of everything you desire. You are made for more than enough. Do not settle for less. Receive the large portion of the Lord. Amen.

Lord, I thank You, for You are my portion. I receive Your portion of peace, joy, grace, wisdom, health, life and godliness in Jesus' name.
Amen.

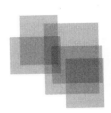

Day 235
The Lord is Good

"The Lord is good to those who wait for Him, to the soul who seeks Him."

Lamentations 3:25

The Lord is good to those who wait on Him, those who keep on believing and those who keep on trusting in Him. Rejection, pain and hurt are no match for the greatness in the inside of you. Keep hoping in faith and keep seeking God. I declare you will experience the goodness of God in your life. Amen.

Lord, I thank You for Your goodness in my life.
Give me the grace to continue to hope in You and to
continue to seek You in Jesus' name.
Amen.

_____

_____

_____

_____

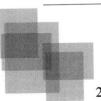

Simple and Powerful Truth to help Jump Start Your Day

Day 236
The Shift

*"...The wealth of the sinner is
stored up for the righteous."*

Proverbs 13:22

Because you have chosen to trust in God and you are doing your best to
live your life to honor him, He will shift you from barely making it in
every area of your life to having more than enough. He will shift the wealth
of the sinners into your storehouse. A shift is coming into your life. Amen.

*Lord, I thank You for Your shift in my life. I thank
You that You are shifting from lack to abundance,
from sickness to health, from grace to grace, from
peace to peace and from joy to joy in Jesus' name.
Amen.*

_____

_____

_____

_____

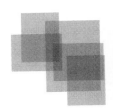

Day 237
A Thousand More

"May the Lord God of your fathers make you a thousand times more numerous than you are, and bless you as He has promised you!"

Deuteronomy 1:11

God has blessed you before in the past, but He wants to amaze you with His blessings. He wants to give you a thousand times more joy, peace, favor, health, good relationships and prosperity. Your best is yet to come. Believe and receive this into your life. Amen.

Lord, I thank You for what You have done in my life, for what You are doing and for what You are going to do. I thank You for a thousand more of everything that pertains to life and godliness in Jesus' name.
Amen.

_____

_____

_____

_____

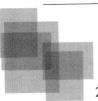

Simple and Powerful Truth to help Jump Start Your Day

Day 238
Walk with the Wise

"He who walks with wise men will be wise, but the companion of fools will be destroyed."

Proverbs 13:20

You are designed and destined for greatness; remember not everyone is right for you. Associate with wise people who will make your greatness come alive. You are blessed and highly favored. I declare right people are coming across your path. Amen.

Lord, weed the wrong people out of my life and bring the right people into my life. I thank You for Your wisdom to walk the wise in Jesus' name. Amen.

_____

_____

_____

_____

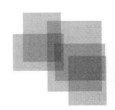

Day 239
Agree with God!

"Then Mary said, 'Behold the
maidservant of the Lord! Let it be
to me according to your word.'"

Luke 1:38

God has promised to bless you. Just like Mary agreed with God, agree with God today about His promises for your life. Amen.

Lord, give me the grace to agree with Your promises
for every area of my life in Jesus' name.
Amen.

_____

_____

_____

_____

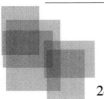

Simple and Powerful Truth to help Jump Start Your Day

Day 240
Be Like A Deer!

"As the deer pants for the water brooks, So pants my soul for You, O God."

Psalms 42:1

Your soul is your depth of who you are here on earth. Your emotion, personality, passion, feelings, compassion and empathy are all shaped and formed from within your soul. How good is your soul? Be like a deer. Let your soul long for God; let your soul be saturated with the promises and the goodness of God. Amen.

Lord, give me the grace to feed my soul with Your promises and with Your goodness in Jesus' name. Amen.

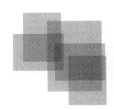

Day 241
Your End Is Great

"Declaring the end from the beginning, and from ancient times the things that are not yet done, saying, My counsel shall stand, and I will do all my pleasure."

Isaiah 46:10

God already knows the end of your story. The end of that situation confronting you is peace, joy, abundance, grace and freedom. Do not give up because of how difficult that situation seems. Instead, let hope rise up on the inside of you. God already declared you victorious. Amen.

Lord, give me the grace to enjoy the journey on my way to the good things You have in store for every area of my life in Jesus' name.
Amen.

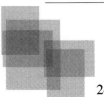

Simple and Powerful Truth to help Jump Start Your Day

Day 242
Daily Loads of Blessings!

"Blessed be the Lord,
Who daily loads us with benefits,
the God of our salvation!"

Psalms 68:19

God is blessings you with loads of benefits daily. That means you have everything you need to have a successful day. Do not allow fear or a situation to prevent you from enjoying these daily loads of benefits. Receive His daily loads of benefits into your life today. Wake up every morning expecting the loads of God's benefits. Amen.

Lord, I thank You for Your daily loads of benefits.
Give me the grace to receive them daily into my
life in Jesus' name.
Amen.

_____

_____

_____

_____

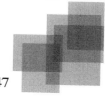

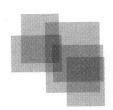

Day 243
Something Good

"For the Lord God is a sun and shield; The Lord will give grace and glory; No good thing will He withhold from those who walk uprightly."

Psalms 84:11

Expect something good to happen to you today. God wants to be good to you. He promises not to withhold anything that is good from you. That situation does not match the goodness of our God. I am in agreement with you that something good will happen to you today. Amen.

Lord, do something good in my life today in
Jesus' name.
Amen.

_____

_____

_____

_____

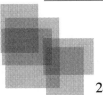

Simple and Powerful Truth to help Jump Start Your Day

Day 244
He'll Never Fail

*"Be strong and of good courage,
do not fear nor be afraid of them;
for the Lord your God, He is the
One who goes with you. He will
not leave you nor forsake you."*

Deuteronomy 31:6

God has not failed before and He is not going to fail or disappoint you. Surrender to Him and allow His strength to flow into your life. Do not be timid, because of a situation or a person causing you trouble. Be strong and courageous and keep hoping on in faith. Your breakthroughs are in sight. He will never fail you. Amen.

*Lord, I thank you for being on my side and for
fighting my battles for me. Give me the grace to
be strong and courageous in the face of difficult
situation in Jesus' name.
Amen.*

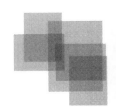

Day 245
The Completion

*"Being confident of this very thing,
that He who has begun a good
work in you will complete it until
the day of Jesus Christ."*

Philippians 1:6

God has started a good work in your life and He promise to complete it.
The end of your story is abundance of everything that is good. Sickness is
completed with health and healing, financial difficulty is completed with an
abundance of prosperity, a difficult situation is completed with victory.
Do not give up your hope; God is working on your behalf, and His
blessings are abounding in your life. Amen.

*Lord, give me the grace to not be distracted by a
person or situation from the good work You are
completing in every area of my life. I trust in You
in Jesus' name.
Amen.*

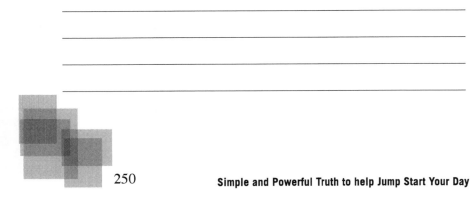

Simple and Powerful Truth to help Jump Start Your Day

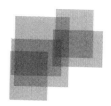

Day 246
God of Wonders

*"For You are great,
and do wondrous things;
You alone are God."*

Psalms 86:10

Our God is a God of wonders. He will turn your scares into stars, He will turn your tests, trials and tribulations into testimonies, He will turn your sorrow into joy and He will turn your mourning into dancing. Suddenly, you will experience victory and breakthroughs in your life and relationships. Amen.

*I declare you will experience the wondrous power
of God in every area your life in Jesus' name.
Amen.*

_____

_____

_____

_____

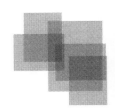

Day 247
He Is Lord

*"The Lord is near to those who
have a broken heart, and saves
such as have a contrite spirit."*

Psalms 34:18

God is Lord and He is your Lord. He is Lord over that situation confronting
you and He is saying, "I've got this." Nothing catches Him by surprise.
Keep doing your best, keep on trusting, and keep on hoping in Him.
He is Lord! Amen.

*Lord, I thank You that You are my Lord and Lord
over every situation confronting me. I give You
praise and I trust in You in Jesus' name.
Amen.*

Simple and Powerful Truth to help Jump Start Your Day

Day 248
You Will Cross Over!

*"...All Israel CROSSED over
on dry ground, until all the
people had crossed completely
over the Jordan."*

Joshua 3:17

Your victories are in sight. You will cross over from sorrow to joy, from mourning to dancing. You will cross to peace, abundance, prosperity, good health and divine favor in your life and relationships. That pain is coming to an end; you are crossing over. Amen.

*Lord, I thank You for giving me the grace to
cross over into the fullness of Your joy and Your
abundance of blessings for every area of my life in
Jesus' name.
Amen.*

Day 249
Be Strong

"Watch, stand fast in the faith,
be brave, be strong."

1 Corinthians 16:13

When we keep living, there will be rejections, loss, pain, failures, mistakes and setbacks. If you stay strong in the Lord and if you do not lose hope, your story will end in success. That situation might create temporary setbacks, but your comebacks are in sight. Be strong! Amen

Lord, give me the grace to be brave and strong in
the face of difficult situations. Help me to not lose
hope but to consistently trust in You, in Jesus' name.
Amen.

Day 250
He Knows Everything About You

"But the very hairs of your head are all numbered. Do not fear therefore; you are of more value than many sparrows."

Luke 12:7

Whatever concerns you concerns God. He is longing to be good to you. He knows everything about you and He knows the numbers of your hair. My friend, you need not worry about that situation; you need to trust in God and give thanks for your miracles. Amen.

Lord, I thank You that You know everything about me. Give me the grace to trust in You to see me through to my success and victory in every area of my life in Jesus' name.
Amen.

_____

_____

_____

_____

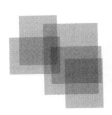

Day 251
God Has Delivered

*"And they said to Joshua,
'Truly the Lord has DELIVERED all
the land into our hands, for indeed
all the inhabitants of the country are
fainthearted because of us.'"*

Joshua 2:24

God has delivered to you everything you need to be successful in every area of your life. Just open the package by believing, trusting and claiming what He has delivered to you. Amen.

*Lord, give me the grace to keep on believing,
trusting and claiming Your promises for every area
of my life in Jesus' name.
Amen.*

_____

_____

_____

_____

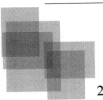

Simple and Powerful Truth to help Jump Start Your Day

Day 252
Consecrate Yourself

And Joshua said to the people,
'Sanctify (CONSECRATE)
yourselves, for tomorrow the Lord
will do WONDERS among you.'"

Joshua 3:5

Take some time once a week to fast and pray. Learn about fasting and consecrating yourself to the Lord. God wants to do wonders in your life, and one of the purposes of fasting is to help move you closer to God. You will not miss your opportunity in Jesus' name. Amen.

Lord, give me the grace and the wisdom to fast,
to consecrate myself to You. I want to know You
more and more in Jesus' name.
Amen.

Day 253
Redeemed

*"In Him we have redemption
through His blood, the forgiveness
of sins, according to the riches
of His grace."*

Ephesians 1:7

You have been redeemed by the blood of Jesus Christ, forgiven of your past, present and future sins. You have riches beyond measure for every area of your life by His grace. You have been redeemed into the richness of His grace. Amen.

*Lord, I thank You for I have been redeemed. Give me
the grace to enjoy Your full redemption in every area
of my life in Jesus' name.
Amen.*

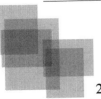

Simple and Powerful Truth to help Jump Start Your Day

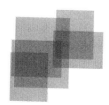

Day 254
Use Your Authority

*"Assuredly, I say to you, whatever
you bind on earth will be bound
in heaven, and whatever you
loose on earth will be loosed in
heaven."*

Matthew 18:18

You have it in you to win and succeed in every area of your life. Instead of using your mind to worry, use your mind to create the impossible. Meditate on and declare the promises of God over that situation. You are empowered and equipped to be victorious. Use your authority. Amen.

*Lord, give me the grace to use the authority
You have given me for the advancement of Your
kingdom, for the benefits of others and for my
benefits in Jesus' name.
Amen.*

_____

_____

_____

_____

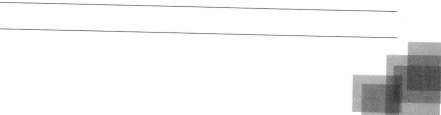

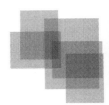

Day 255
He's Your Vindicator

"The Lord will fight for you,
and you shall hold your peace."

Exodus 14:14

God knows the wrong that has been done to you, the hurtful things that were said about you, the betrayal and the belittling. He is telling you to hold your peace and that He will fight your battles for you. He is your vindicator and He will never let you down. Amen.

Lord, I surrender the pain, hurt and disappointments
to you. I thank You, for You alone are my vindicator
in Jesus' name.
Amen.

_____

_____

_____

_____

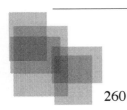

Simple and Powerful Truth to help Jump Start Your Day

Day 256
Your Home, His Home

"Jesus answered and said to him, 'If anyone loves Me, he will keep My word; and My Father will love him, and We will come to him and make Our home with him.'"

John 14:23

When you choose to live your life to honor God daily you are showing your love to our Heavenly Father, and He will make your home His dwelling place. What is your level of love for God? He is longing to make your home His home. When God makes your home His dwelling place, your home will be filled with peace, joy, abundance and all kinds of good things. Amen.

Lord, give me the grace to live my life to honor You, I thank You for making my home Your dwelling place in Jesus' name.
Amen.

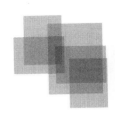

Day 257
Serve Through Love

"For you, brethren, have been called to liberty; only do not use liberty as an opportunity for the flesh, but through love serve one another."

Galatians 5:13

How do you serve in different areas of your life? What is the basis of your service to others? You have the liberty to serve the people in your life and others through love. When you do, God will diligently reward you. Amen.

*Lord, give me the grace to serve the people in my life
and others through Your love in Jesus' name.
Amen.*

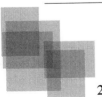

Simple and Powerful Truth to help Jump Start Your Day

Day 258
Open the Door

Behold, I stand at the door and knock. If anyone hears My voice and opens the door, I will come in to him and dine with him, and he with Me.

Revelation 3:20

God wants to dine with you. He wants to bless your house and your life. God is telling you to open the door for peace, joy, happiness, healing, righteousness, salvation and abundance. Open the door; He is knocking and ready to overflow your life with His goodness. Amen.

Lord, give me the grace to open the door to
everything that pertains to a life and godliness
when You knock in Jesus' name.
Amen.

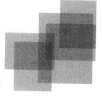

Day 259
Be Strong in The Lord

*"Finally, my brethren, be strong
in the Lord and in the power
of His might."*

Ephesians 6:10

Be strong not in your own power, faith or wisdom, but in the Lord.
When you are strong in the Lord through meditating on His word, praying
and fasting, praising and giving thanks and declaring His promises over
your life, His wisdom, faith, favor, protection, healing, prosperity and
power will become yours. Amen.

*I declare that I am strong in the Lord and in the
Power of His might. No weapon formed against me
shall prosper. I live my life in the goodness of God
in Jesus' name.
Amen.*

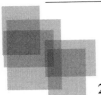

Simple and Powerful Truth to help Jump Start Your Day

Day 260
No More Reproach

"Then the Lord said to Joshua, 'This day I have rolled away the reproach of Egypt from you.' Therefore the name of the place is called Gilgal to this day."

Joshua 5:9

I declare that the reproach of generational curse, sickness, depression, poverty, lack and bondage are rolled away from your life and from your family. I declare that your life is being infused with the power and the grace of God. No more reproach in Jesus' name. Amen.

Lord, I thank You for taking away any reproach in my life. I live in Your glorious power in Jesus' name. Amen.

_____

_____

_____

_____

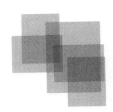

Day 261
The Captain

*"And he said, Nay; but as
CAPTAIN of the host of the Lord
am I now come. And Joshua fell
on his face to the earth, and did
worship, and said unto him, what
saith my Lord unto his servant?*
Joshua 5:14 (KJV)

Make the Lord the Captain of your life, home, job, business and everything
that pertains to your life. When the Lord is leading and guiding you and
when you follow His leading and His guidance, your victory is assured.
Say, "Lord, be the Captain of my life." Amen.

*Lord, I surrender my life to You. I ask You to be the
Captain of my life and my home. Lead me, guide me
and make me in Jesus' name.
Amen.*

_____

_____

_____

_____

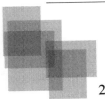

Simple and Powerful Truth to help Jump Start Your Day

Day 262
Shout!

"And the seventh time it happened, when the priests blew the trumpets, that Joshua said to the people: 'SHOUT, for the Lord has given you the city!'"

Joshua 6:16

You have been praying over that situation long enough; now is the time to shout for joy, victory and your breakthrough. Our Lord is Lord over that situation confronting you. Shout for the Lord has given you what you have been believing for. It is time to shout and give thanks to the Lord for His goodness in Jesus' name. Amen.

Lord, give me the grace to shout for victory in the midst of that difficulty. Lord, I thank You for Your goodness and for filling my mouth with the shout of praise in Jesus' name.
Amen.

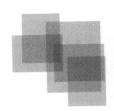

Day 263
Shout for Joy!

*"Let them SHOUT FOR JOY
and be glad, who favor my
righteous cause; And let them
say continually, 'Let the Lord be
magnified, Who has pleasure in
the prosperity of His servant.'"*

Psalms 35:27

When you live your life to honor God daily, you need to shout for joy and be glad. God has a great pleasure in prospering every area of your life, my friend. Expect the prosperity of our Lord in every area of your life. God wants to magnify Himself in your life. Praise God!

*Lord, magnify Your blessings, abundance, health,
wisdom and everything that pertains to life and
goodliness in every area of my life in Jesus' name.
Amen.*

_____

_____

_____

_____

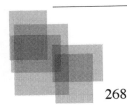

Simple and Powerful Truth to help Jump Start Your Day

Day 264
Fame

*"So the Lord was with Joshua,
and his FAME spread throughout
all the country."*

Joshua 6:27

Our Lord is with you; keep doing your best to live your life to honor God. Your fame will soon be made manifest in your family, on your job, in your business, in your community and in the world. You are set for greatness. Praise God!

*Lord, I thank You, for You are with me, and I thank
You for making Your glory fill every area of my life
in Jesus' name.
Amen.*

_____

_____

_____

_____

Day 265
No More Valley of Trouble

"...Therefore the name of that
place has been called the Valley
of Achor (Trouble) to this day."

Joshua 7:26

I declare you will have the grace to overcome valleys of trouble in your health, finances, physically, mentally, and in your relationships. You are not going under, you are going over that situation and everything that is holding you back. Praise God! Amen.

Lord, I thank you for Your victory over any valleys
of trouble in every area of my life. I thank you
for guiding me through this difficult situation in
Jesus' name.
Amen.

_____

_____

_____

_____

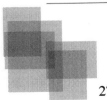

Simple and Powerful Truth to help Jump Start Your Day

Day 266
Covenant Keeper

"Therefore know that the Lord your God, He is God, the faithful God who keeps covenant and mercy for a thousand generations with those who love Him and keep His commandments."

Deuteronomy 7:9

When you chose to live your life to honor God daily, He promises to keep His covenant of peace, joy, abundance, good health and prosperity in your life. When you fall, get back up and God will keep His covenant of forgiveness and blessings in your life. He is a covenant keeping God. Amen.

Lord, I thank You, for You are a covenant keeping God. Give me the grace to live in Your covenant of peace, joy, health, wisdom and abundance in Jesus' name.
Amen.

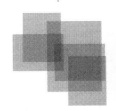

Day 267
The Living Hope

"Blessed be the God and Father
of our Lord Jesus Christ, who
according to His abundant mercy
has begotten us again to a LIVING
HOPE through the resurrection of
Jesus Christ from the dead."

1 Peter 1:3 NKJV

You can put your hope in a doctor's report, a friend, spouse, job, business or your strength, but your hope can be dashed. Put your hope in God; He is the living hope. He will keep your hope alive and turn your hope into reality. Hope in God to overcome that situation and to accomplish your heart desires. Amen.

Lord, I thank You, for you are my living hope.
Give me the grace to continually hope in You
in Jesus' name.
Amen.

_____

_____

_____

_____

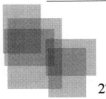

272

Day 268
He's Not Resting

"Have you not known?
Have you not heard?
The everlasting God, the Lord the
Creator of the ends of the earth,
neither faints nor is weary.
His understanding is
unsearchable."

Isaiah 40:28

God knows everything about you and He is not surprised about the situation confronting you. He is not resting concerning you, He understands your pain and knows what you need. Put your hope and trust in him, for He loves you. He is rooting for you. You are not going under. Amen.

Lord, I thank You, for You are on my side and
rooting for my victory. I trust in You for my victory
and breakthrough in Jesus' name.
Amen.

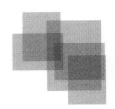

Day 269
One Thing

"One thing I have desired of the Lord, That will I seek: That I may dwell in the house of the Lord All the days of my life, To behold the beauty of the Lord, And to inquire in His temple."

Psalms 27:4

If there is only one thing to desire, it should be the grace to make God the first priority in your life. Serve God diligently with your time and resources. When you do, He will reveal Himself to you, guide you and make His blessings abound in every area of your life. Amen.

Lord, give me the grace to put You first in every area of my life. Give me the grace to dwell in the fullness of Your grace daily in Jesus' name.
Amen.

_____

_____

_____

_____

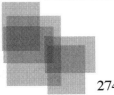

Simple and Powerful Truth to help Jump Start Your Day

Day 270
More Blessing

*"...And remember the words of the
Lord Jesus, that He said,
'It is MORE BLESSED to give
than to receive.'"*

Acts 20:35

In giving you will receive. When you give more, you will receive more. Give away what you want in any area of your life, no matter how small it is. You get more blessings by giving, and it is more of a blessing to give than to receive. Amen.

*Lord, I thank You for a heart of giving my time,
money and resources to benefit others. I thank You
for the abundance of Your blessings in my life in
Jesus' name.
Amen.*

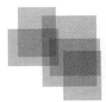

Day 271
You Have the Victory

"But thanks be to God,
who gives us the victory through
our Lord Jesus Christ."

1 Corinthians 15:57

God already gave you the victory over that sin, addiction, sickness, lack, relationship problem and anything that is holding you back. Nothing is wrong with you; you might have an issue, but you also have the victory of God over that issue. Instead of worrying over that situation, give thanks for your victory over that situation. Amen.

Lord, I thank You for Your victory in my life. I
declare that I am victory bound in Jesus' name.
Amen.

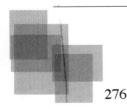

Simple and Powerful Truth to help Jump Start Your Day

Day 272
You Have the Gift

"For the wages of sin is death,
but the gift of God is eternal life
in Christ Jesus our Lord."

Romans 6:23

Do not allow repeated sin to hold you down. If you commit the same sin again and again, do not feel condemned. Get back up and receive God's forgiveness and ask Him to help you to do better next time. You have the gifts of eternal life, freedom, salvation, health, wisdom and abundance. Amen.

Lord, I thank You for Your gift of Eternal life. I
thank You for Your freedom, peace, joy, abundance
and grace to overcome in Jesus' name.
Amen.

_____

_____

_____

_____

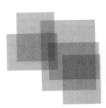

Day 272
The Lord Has Spoken

"He will swallow up death forever,
And the Lord God will wipe away
tears from all faces;
The rebuke of His people He will
take away from all the earth;
For the Lord has spoken."

Isaiah 25:8

Your sorrow is coming to an end, your tears of sadness will be turned to tears of joy and your shame shall be turned to glory. The Lord has spoken victory, health, peace, wisdom, protection, grace and abundance into your life. Amen.

Lord, I thank You for speaking Your goodness into
my life. Give me the grace to receive Your promises
into my life in Jesus' name.
Amen.

_____

_____

_____

_____

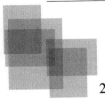

Simple and Powerful Truth to help Jump Start Your Day

Day 274
You're Saved!

"For God did not send His Son into the world to condemn the world, but that the world through Him might be saved."

John 3:17

No matter what, you are not condemned; you are saved from sickness, pain, sorrow, lacks and anything that is holding you back. Whatever you are going through is temporary. Start taking baby steps and have faith in the saving grace of God. Amen.

Lord, I thank You for my salvation. I thank You
that
I abound in Your saving grace in Jesus' name.
Amen.

Day 275
The Demonstrations of Love

"But God demonstrates
His own love toward us,
in that while we were still sinners,
Christ died for us."

Romans 5:8

Jesus Christ paid it all; He paid for your sins before you committed them,
He paid for your health before you get sick, He paid for your prosperity
and for everything you will ever need. He did it not because of you,
but in spite of you. This is the demonstration of His of love toward us!
Amen.

Lord, I thank You for the demonstrations of Your love
towards me. I thank You for Your unconditional love.
Give me the grace to abound in Your love
in Jesus' name.
Amen.

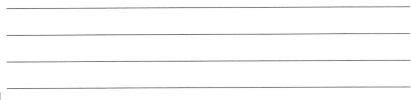

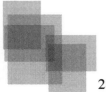

Simple and Powerful Truth to help Jump Start Your Day

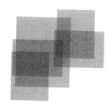

Day 276
It's Temporary

"Jesus said to her,
'I am the resurrection and the life.
He who believes in Me, though
he may die, he shall live. And
whoever lives and believes in Me
shall never die. Do you believe
this?'"

John 11:25-26

You might have some challenges in different areas of your life. Things might seem dead, but it is temporary, because you are in Christ, His resurrection and power will breathe life into that situation. Arise, for it is temporary. Amen.

Lord, I thank You for Your resurrection and power
working in my life and for causing me to triumph
in every area of my life in Jesus' name.
Amen.

_____

_____

_____

_____

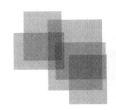

Day 277
No More Bondage

"But He was wounded for our
transgressions, He was bruised for
our iniquities; The chastisement for
our peace was upon Him,
And by His stripes we are healed."

Isaiah 53:5

Jesus Christ has paid for your salvation, healing and everything you will ever need in every area of your life. No bondage can hold you back. You are free, because of Jesus. Trust in Him today and receive His complete work of abundance He has in store for you. Amen.

Lord, thank You for Your healing, freedom and
deliverance in every area of my life in Jesus' name.
Amen.

_____

_____

_____

_____

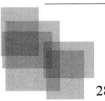

Day 278
The Spirit of Him

"But if the Spirit of Him who raised Jesus from the dead dwells in you, He who raised Christ from the dead will also give life to your mortal bodies through His Spirit who dwells in you."

Romans 8:11

You are not going under, you are going over the top. There is no stopping you; no one and no situation is a match for our God. Every dead thing in every area of your life must come to life, because you have the same Spirit that raised Christ from the dead on the inside of you. Let hope rise up on the inside of you. Arise and shine. Amen.

Lord, I thank You for Your resurrection and power in my life. Give me the grace to live in the reality of this power in Jesus' name.
Amen.

Day 279
The Manifested Love

"In this the love of God was
manifested toward us,
that God has sent His only begotten
Son into the world, that we might
live through Him."

1 John 4:9

God manifested His love towards you by giving His only son to die for your sins, salvation, health and prosperity in every area of your life. When facing a difficult situation, remember that God loves you and He wants to help you. Reach out to Him. Amen.

Lord, I thank You for manifesting Your love toward
me. Lord, give me grace to live Your love with honor
in Jesus' name.
Amen,

_____

_____

_____

_____

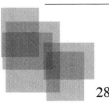

Simple and Powerful Truth to help Jump Start Your Day

Day 280
The Name of the Lord

"And it shall come to pass that whoever calls on the name of the Lord Shall be saved."

Acts 2:21

The name of the Lord has the power to save, deliver, set free, empower, restore and prosper. Whatever it is that is confronting you today is no match for the power in the name of our Lord and Savior Jesus Christ. Just say, "In the name of Jesus…" Amen.

Lord, I thank You for the power in Your name.
Give me the grace to consistently call on Your name in Jesus' name.
Amen.

_____

_____

_____

_____

Day 281
He Always Direct Right

"A man's heart plans his way,
But the Lord directs his steps."

Proverbs 16:9

Plan, set goals and take positive actions, but never forget to let God direct your steps. He always directs right. He leads to success, health, restoration and abundance for everything that is good.

Lord, I surrender all to You. Lead, guide and direct
my steps in Jesus' name.
Amen.

_____

_____

_____

_____

Simple and Powerful Truth to help Jump Start Your Day

Day 282
The Spirit of the Lord

"Now the Lord is the Spirit;
and where the Spirit of the Lord
is, there is liberty."

2 Corinthians 3:17

If you have received Jesus Christ as your personal Lord and Savior, you have the Spirit of the Lord on the inside of you. That Spirit produces freedom, health, prosperity, wisdom, grace and liberty in your life. Recognize who you are; you are a powerhouse. Amen.

Lord, I thank You for Your spirit in my life.
Give me the grace to enjoy the benefits of Your
Spirit in my life in Jesus' name.
Amen.

_____

_____

_____

_____

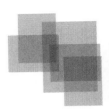

Day 283
Stand in His Liberty!

"Stand fast therefore in the liberty
by which Christ has made us free,
and do not be entangled again with
a yoke of bondage."

Galatians 5:1

When Jesus died and was resurrected, He did it for your healing, salvation and for everything that is good in life. God is simple. He said, "Ask and you will receive..." Do not get entangled in religion innuendos. You cannot do anything to earn His love and you cannot do anything to lose His love. Stand fast in this liberty. Amen.

Lord, I thank You for the simplicity of Your
relationships with me. Give me the grace not to
entangle myself with any religion innuendos.
I live my life to honor You in Jesus' name.
Amen.

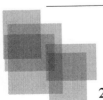

Simple and Powerful Truth to help Jump Start Your Day

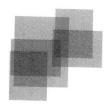

Day 284
In Christ

"But now in Christ Jesus
you who once were far off have
been brought near by the
blood of Christ"

Ephesians 2:1

The blood of Christ gives you unlimited access to our Heavenly Father. You have access to peace, health, grace, forgiveness and incredible blessings for your daily need. You are not far away. You are in Christ and in Him you have all things. Amen.

Lord, I thank You for bringing me close to
You through Christ Jesus. Give me the grace to
enjoy all the benefits in the fullness of my Lord and
Savior Jesus Christ in Jesus' name.
Amen.

_____

_____

_____

_____

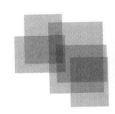

Day 285
Avoid Neglect

"Then Joshua said to the children of Israel: 'How long will you NEGLECT to go and possess the land which the Lord God of your fathers has given you?'"

Joshua 18:3

God gave you everything you will ever need when He sent Jesus to die for you. When you need peace, wisdom, mercy, favor or healing, you should rise up and possess them. When you worry and allow fear, you are neglecting all the benefits God already gave to you. Amen.

Lord, give me the grace not to neglect Your promises in my life. Give me the grace to arise and possess Your promises in my life in Jesus' name.
Amen.

_____

_____

_____

_____

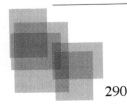

Simple and Powerful Truth to help Jump Start Your Day

Day 286
When You Trust in the Lord...

"The fear of man brings a snare,
but whoever trusts in the Lord
shall be safe."

Proverbs 29:25

Trusting in the Lord will lead you to be fearless of what anyone can do to you or of any situation. When you trust in the Lord, He will protect you, help you, guide you, and keep your mind at peace. Trust in the Lord consistently. Amen.

Lord, give me the grace to trust in You
consistently. I thank You for victory over fear in
Jesus' name. Amen.

_____

_____

_____

_____

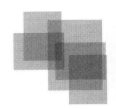

Day 287
His Good Pleasure

*"For it is God who works in
you both to will and to do for
His good pleasure."*

Philippians 2:13

The good pleasure of our Lord is for you to thrive, not survive, and for you to be the head, above, strong and full of life. He is causing you to rise to the top in every area of your life. You are not alone; God is with you causing you to prosper. You just need to follow His leading. Amen.

*Lord, I thank You for working in every area of my
life both to will and to do Your good pleasure.
I receive the abundance of Your blessings in my life
in Jesus' name.
Amen.*

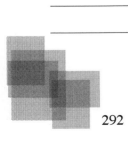

Simple and Powerful Truth to help Jump Start Your Day

Day 288
Choose Your Battle Wisely

*"Even a fool is counted wise when
he holds his peace;
When he shuts his lips,
he is considered perceptive."*

Proverbs 17:28

Choose your battle wisely! You do not have to respond to every critic and to the naysayers. Sometimes you have to hold your peace and let God fight your battles for you. Focus on your destiny. You have a great future in front of you; do not allow small-minded people to distract you from the divine plan of God for your life. Amen.

*Lord, give me the wisdom to choose my battle
wisely. I thank You for Your peace in my life in
Jesus' name. Amen.*

_____

_____

_____

_____

Day 289
Everything Rises and Falls on You

"For all the law is fulfilled in one word, even in this: 'You shall love your neighbor as yourself.'"

Galatians 5:14

Everything rises and falls on you. If you do not love yourself, you cannot love the people in your life. You cannot give what you do not have. Allow the love of God to flow into you and through you to others. Do you love yourself? Amen.

Lord, give me the grace to love myself. I receive Your love into my life and I thank You that Your love is flowing through me to others in Jesus' name. Amen.

_____
_____
_____
_____

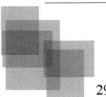

Simple and Powerful Truth to help Jump Start Your Day

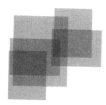

Day 290
Accept One Another

"Therefore receive one another,
just as Christ also received us,
to the glory of God."

Romans 15:7

Accept your friends, family members and co-workers, but do not allow their weaknesses, bad habits and shortcomings to affect you. Some family members, friends and co-workers will have to be loved from a distance. It is not because you are better; you just want a better life for you and your family. Amen.

Lord, give me the grace to accept others in love in
Jesus' name.
Amen.

_____

_____

_____

_____

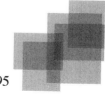

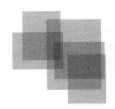

Day 291
Do Not Forget

*"But do not forget to do good
and to share, for with such
sacrifices God is well pleased."*

Hebrews 13:16

The scripture says, "Do not forget to do good and to share." That means there is a possibility to forget to do good and to share. Be intentional about doing good and sharing with others. God is well pleased with this act, and it equals a galore of blessings for you. Amen.

*Lord, give me the grace to do good and to share
Your blessings in my life with others in Jesus' name.
Amen.*

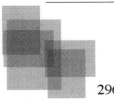

296

Day 292
Not Your Understanding

"Trust in the Lord with all your heart, And lean not on your own understanding."

Proverbs 3:5

Your understanding of that situation is limited, but God has all understandings of what you are going through. He is asking you to trust in Him and not lean on your own understanding. He knows and He wants to help you. Amen.

Lord, give me the grace not to lean on my own understanding. Help me to trust in Your guidance in Jesus' name.
Amen.

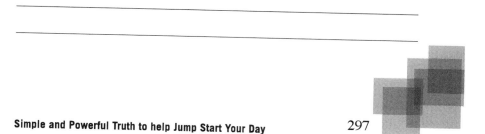

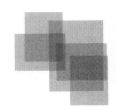

Day 293
Acknowledge Him

*"In all your ways acknowledge
Him, And He shall direct
your paths."*

Proverbs 3:6

Acknowledge God in the small and big things of life. He is concerned about anything that concerns you; instead of worrying about that situation, acknowledge God and ask Him to help you. He will direct your paths. Amen.

*Lord, give me the grace to acknowledge You in all
my ways and dealings in Jesus' name.
Amen.*

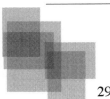

Simple and Powerful Truth to help Jump Start Your Day

Day 294
The Only Fear Allowed

"The fear of the Lord
is the beginning of wisdom..."

Proverbs 9:10

The only fear you are allowed to have is the fear of the Lord. The fear of the Lord is your desire to live your life to honor Him daily. Live your life to honor God, not in fear but in honor of who He is and what He has done in your life, and you will be filled with wisdom in every aspect of your life. Amen.

Lord, give me the grace to live my life in Your
reverential fear. I thank You for Your wisdom in
my life in Jesus' name.
Amen.

_____

_____

_____

_____

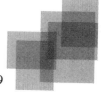

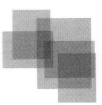

Day 295
The Results of Righteousness

*"The work of righteousness
will be peace, and the effect of
righteousness, quietness and
assurance forever."*

Isaiah 32:17

Living a righteous life is not living a perfect life; it means intentionally relying on the grace of God to live your daily life to honor Him. When you sin, you receive His forgiveness in your life, because you choose to live a righteous life. Living a righteous life will give you an experience of peace, quietness and assurance for every area of your life. Amen.

*Lord, give me the grace to live a righteous life.
I thank You that all the benefits of righteousness are
abounding in my life in Jesus' name.
Amen.*

_____

_____

_____

_____

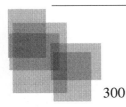

Simple and Powerful Truth to help Jump Start Your Day

Day 296
Only God Can Satisfy!

*"Until now you have asked
nothing in My name. Ask,
and you will receive, that your
joy may be full."*

John 16:24

No one or anything can satisfy you more than God. Do not look for satisfaction in a person or in a thing. Ask God in faith for help concerning that relationship, addiction, bad habit, or that situation. He will fill you with joy and the grace to overcome. Trust in Him today to satisfy every need in your life. Amen.

*Lord, I thank you, for You alone can satisfy
me. Lord, give me the grace to only seek my
satisfaction in You in Jesus' name.
Amen.*

Day 297
The Beginning and the End

" 'I am the Alpha and the Omega,
the Beginning and the End,'
says the Lord, 'who is and who was
and who is to come, the Almighty.' "

Revelation 1:8

Before you go through any situation, God already knows the end of that situation. The end of it is peace, joy, abundance, freedom, health and breakthrough. Do not allow the enemy, fear, doubt and unbelief to change your ending. God is the beginning and the end. He knows; trust in Him. Amen.

Lord, I surrender all to You. Be the beginning and
the ending of my life. I trust in You for my victory
and breakthrough in Jesus' name.
Amen.

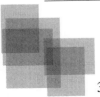

Simple and Powerful Truth to help Jump Start Your Day

Day 298
Created For Good Works

"For we are His workmanship, created in Christ Jesus for good works, which God prepared beforehand that we should walk in them."

Ephesians 2:10

You are created to produce goods. You have the seed of greatness on the inside of you. You have it in you to win. You are destined for greatness. Do not allow temporary situations to define your life. Walk in the greatness God has put in you. Amen.

Lord, give me the grace to live in the greatness You destined for me. I thank You that You are causing me to produce abundance of goods in my life in Jesus' name.
Amen.

Day 299
Let His Peace Rule Your Heart

"And let the peace of God rule
in your hearts, to which also you
were called in one body;
and be thankful."

Colossians 3:15

Do not allow fear, doubt and unbelief to rule your heart. Do not allow your mistakes, rejections and setbacks to rule your heart. Be thankful for your victory and allow the peace of God rule your heart. Amen.

Lord, give me the grace to allow Your peace to rule
in my heart in Jesus' name.
Amen.

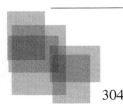

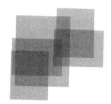

Day 300
He Will Hold You

"If I say, 'My foot slips,'
Your mercy, O Lord,
will hold me up."

Psalms 94:18

No matter how far or how low you have gone, the mercy of God will hold you up. When you fall, rely on His mercy to see you through and to cause you to overcome. He is faithful and He will never leave you without help. Amen.

Lord, I thank You that Your mercy is holding me.
Give me the grace to live in the reality of Your
mercy holding me in Jesus' name.
Amen.

_____

_____

_____

_____

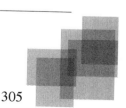

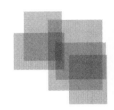

Day 301
His Comforts

*"In the multitude of my
anxieties within me,
Your comforts delight my soul."*

Psalms 94:19

God is not surprised about that situation confronting you. He loves you
and He wants to delight you with His comforts and with His goodness in
the midst of that difficulty. Stop worrying and start trusting God for
your victory. Amen.

*Lord, delight me with Your comfort. I thank You
for Your victory over any anxieties in my life
in Jesus' name.
Amen.*

_____

_____

_____

_____

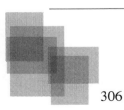

Simple and Powerful Truth to help Jump Start Your Day

Day 302
Pursue Goo

"See that no one renders evil for evil to anyone, but always pursue what is good both for yourselves and for all."

1 Thessalonians 5:15

Just keep living. You will be frustrated, talked about, betrayed and disappointed by others. Do not be tempted to get even – let God fight your battles for you. You just keep on pursing good, and before you know it, God will reward you abundantly. Amen.

Lord, give me the grace to pursue good. I thank you for the abundance of Your goods in my life in Jesus' name.
Amen.

_____

_____

_____

_____

Day 303
The Great God

"Therefore You are great,
O Lord God. For there is none
like You, nor is there any
God besides You..."

2 Samuel 7:22

Our God is a Great God and He wants to do great things in every area of your life. Do not make a temporary situation a permanent situation. Do not dwell on how difficult things are; dwell on the greatness of our God. Keep giving Him praise for your victory. Amen.

Lord, give me the grace to dwell in Your greatness.
I thank You for Your victory in every area of my life
in Jesus' name.
Amen.

_____

_____

_____

_____

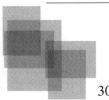

Simple and Powerful Truth to help Jump Start Your Day

Day 304
Focus Your Energy

"So then, my beloved brethren,
let every man be swift to hear,
slow to speak, slow to wrath."

James 1:19

Be swift to praying, reading and studying the Bible. Give thanks, listen to the Holy Spirit and pay attention to people in your life. Be slow to speak, think before you speak, think before making a decision, be slow to anger and choose your battles wisely. Focus your energy. Amen.

Lord, I thank You for the grace to be swift to hear,
slow to speak and slow to anger in all my dealings
in Jesus' name.
Amen.

_____

_____

_____

_____

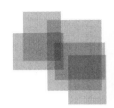

Day 305
The Greatest Gift

"For God so loved the world that
He gave His only begotten Son,
that whoever believes in
Him should not perish
but have everlasting life."

John 3:16

God gave us the greatest gift, Jesus Christ, because He loved us.
Give up your limiting ways, stop limiting your relationships, stop your
habitual sins and receive the greatest gift into your life for free. In Him is
life everlasting, righteousness, peace, joy and every good thing. Amen.

Lord, I receive Your Greatest Gift, Jesus Christ into
my life. Give me the grace to forsake the limiting
things and limiting ways in my life in Jesus' name.
Amen.

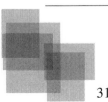

Simple and Powerful Truth to help Jump Start Your Day

Day 306
Cleave

"But you shall hold fast (Cleave)
to the Lord your God,
as you have done to this day."

Joshua 23:8

Do not cleave to depression, worries, anxiety, lacks, sickness, impossibilities or a situation. Instead, cleave to the Lord your God, who has the power over any situation and anything confronting you. He is your Heavenly Father and He is longing to be good to you. Amen.

Lord, I submit this situation into Your hand and
I receive the grace to cleave to You in Jesus' name.
Amen.

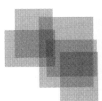

Day 307
When You Call on God

"He shall call upon Me,
and I will answer him;
I will be with him in trouble;
I will deliver him and honor him."

Psalms 91:15

When you call on God, He promises to answer you, He will be with you in times of trouble, He will deliver you and He will honor you with His goodness. Call on God concerning that situation, and He will amaze you with His goodness. Amen.

Lord, give me the grace to consistently call on You
and to consistently give You thanks in Jesus' name.
Amen.

_____

_____

_____

_____

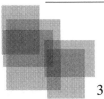

Simple and Powerful Truth to help Jump Start Your Day

Day 308
Please God, Not Others

"And whatever you do in word or deed, do all in the name of the Lord Jesus, giving thanks to God the Father through Him."

Colossians 3:17

If you please others, you will be disappointed, frustrated and miserable. If you please God by what you say and by what you do, others might not like it, but know that you will have peace and be richly blessed by God. Give Him thanks. Amen.

Lord, give me the grace to say and do everything to please you and not others. Fill my mouth with Your praise in Jesus' name.
Amen.

Day 309
You Have It in You to Win

"You are of God, little children,
and have overcome them,
because He who is in you is greater
than he who is in the world."

1 John 4:4

You have it in you to win. God has already deposited everything you need to overcome in you: Himself! Greater is He that is in you than any situation confronting you. Do not allow fear to limit the power on the inside of you. Feed your faith with the word of God. Amen.

Lord, give me the grace to experience the
manifestation of your fullness in my life and grace to
feed my faith with Your word in Jesus' name.
Amen.

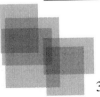

Simple and Powerful Truth to help Jump Start Your Day

Day 310
His Mission

"This is a faithful saying
and worthy of all acceptance,
that Christ Jesus came into
the world to save sinners,
of whom I am chief."

1 Timothy 1:15

The mission and purpose of Jesus Christ was to provide salvation from sins, lacks, sickness and every limitation. Jesus came for you and for every area of your life. Receive Him into your life and allow His mission to become your mission to others. Amen.

Lord, I thank You for my salvation.
Give me the grace to make Your mission my
mission in Jesus' name.
Amen.

Day 311
Joyful shout

"Make a joyful shout to the Lord,
all you lands!"

Psalms 100:1

The situation confronting you is turning around in your favor. Get ready for a shout. Not just any shout, but a joyful shout. This is not the time to give in or give up; this is the time to get your praise on. You are closer to your victory than you think. Make a joyful shout to the Lord. Amen.

Lord, I pray that You will fill my mouth with your
praise and I thank You for causing me to make a
joyful shout unto You in Jesus' name.
Amen.

_____

_____

_____

_____

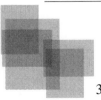

Simple and Powerful Truth to help Jump Start Your Day

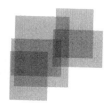

Day 312
Gladness and Singing

"Serve the Lord with gladness;
Come before His presence
with singing."

Psalms 100:2

Serve the Lord with gladness with your giving, praises and worship.
Do not only go to God with your problems, go to His presence with
singing. When your praise goes up, the blessings will come down
abundantly. I am glad that is why I sing. Amen.

Lord, I receive the grace to serve You with
gladness and grace to enter Your presence with
singing in Jesus' name.
Amen.

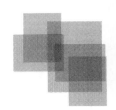

Day 313
Save Your Soul

*"Therefore lay aside all filthiness
and overflow of wickedness,
and receive with meekness the
implanted word, which is able
to save your souls."*

James 1:21

Your soul (mind) comprises your will, emotion and intellect. If your soul is weak, you will have a weak will, emotion and intellect. You will have no will power to move your life forward; save your soul by implanting the word of God into you. Read, study, meditate and confess the word daily over your life. Amen.

*Lord, give me the grace to hunger and thirst after
Your word. Help me to implant Your word with
meekness into my soul in Jesus' name.
Amen.*

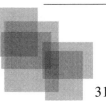

Simple and Powerful Truth to help Jump Start Your Day

Day 314
Be Soft

"A soft answer turns away wrath,
But a harsh word stirs up anger."

Proverbs 15:1

Be soft not with your dreams and passion, but with your responses to people and situations. A soft answer reduces anger, helps you to think before you respond. I encourage you to breathe, think and respond with love and compassion. Amen.

Lord, give me the grace to think and to be at
ease before I respond to situations and people
in Jesus' name.
Amen.

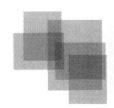

Day 315
My Redeemer Lives

*"For I know that my Redeemer
lives, And He shall stand at last
on the earth."*

Job 19:25

Your Redeemer lives. He lives so you can face tomorrow and any situation confronting you. He lives inside of you and He has redeemed you from curses, lacks, sickness, sin and shame. You have been redeemed. Believe and receive it. Amen.

*Lord, give me the grace to enjoy Your full
redemption power in every area of my life
in Jesus' name.
Amen.*

_____

_____

_____

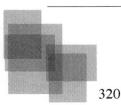

Simple and Powerful Truth to help Jump Start Your Day

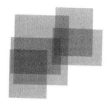

Day 316
By His Stripes

*"...who Himself bore our sins
in His own body on the tree,
that we, having died to sins,
might live for righteousness—
by whose stripes you
were healed."*

1 Peter 2:24

When Jesus died and resurrected, He did it to heal your body, mind and spirit. Jesus did it for every area of your life. Do not let fear of a temporary situation rob you of eternal benefits. By His stripes you are healed. Amen.

*Lord, I thank You for dying for the healing in every
area of my life. Give me the grace to fully enjoy
these eternal benefits in Jesus' name.
Amen.*

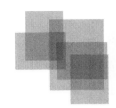

Day 317
Serve The Lord

"And the people said to Joshua,
'No, but we will serve the Lord!'"

Joshua 24:21

Declare today that you will serve the Lord, not your problem, past, lacks, sickness or money. When you serve the Lord, all of these things will bow to you. When you put Him first, He will put you first. Serve Him with your time, money, resources and all your heart. Amen.

Lord, give me the grace to serve with all my might
and with everything I have in Jesus' name.
Amen.

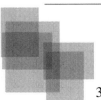

Simple and Powerful Truth to help Jump Start Your Day

Day 318
His Excellency

*"O Lord, our Lord, How excellent
is Your name in all the earth..."*

Psalms 8:1

Our God is an excellent God. He excels over sickness, sorrow, sadness, sins, lacks, demons, wickedness and that situation confronting you. He wants you to excel in every area of your life. His Excellency makes you an excellent person. Do not ever see yourself as not worthy. Amen

*Lord, I thank You for the excellency of
Your name in all the earth. Give me the grace
to fully comprehend Your excellency in my
life in Jesus' name.
Amen.*

Day 319
You Don't Have to Be Consumed

"Through the Lord's mercies
we are not consumed,
Because His compassions fail not."

Lamentations 3:22

You do not have to be consumed by the guilt of sin, depression, anxiety, financial needs, sickness, loss or a situation, because you have the Lord's mercies and His compassions. In the midst of that situation remember the mercies and compassions of our Lord. When the going gets tough, rely on His mercies and compassions. Amen.

Lord, give me the grace to be consumed by
Your mercies and Your compassion, instead of the
situation confronting me in Jesus' name.
Amen,

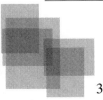

Simple and Powerful Truth to help Jump Start Your Day

Day 320
Daily Supply of Mercies

"Through the Lord's mercies
we are not consumed,
Because His compassions fail not.
They are new every morning;
Great is Your faithfulness."

Lamentations 3:22-23

When you wake up every morning you are waking up to the new mercies of the Lord. God has your back for the day. Do not focus on the troubles of today; focus on the mercies of today. This is your day! Amen.

Lord, give me the grace to focus and rely on
Your mercies for today, in Jesus' name.
Amen.

_____

_____

_____

_____

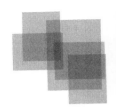

Day 321
He is Your Portion

" 'The Lord is my portion,' says my
soul, 'Therefore I hope in Him!' "

Lamentations 3:24

The Lord is your portion; expect large portions of peace, joy, abundance, favor, good health, wisdom, mercies and compassion. God wants to amaze you with His goodness. You have every reason to hope in Him, since He is your portion.

Lord, I thank You, because You are my portion.
I reject fear and doubt. Lord, give me the grace to
enjoy the portion of everything you have provided
for me in Jesus' name.
Amen.

Simple and Powerful Truth to help Jump Start Your Day

Day 322
Mindset of Love

"You shall love the Lord your God with all your heart, with all your soul, and with all your strength."

Deuteronomy 6:5

Loving God does not mean you will have a perfect life without sins, mistakes and failures. You will have them, and they will be of no surprise to God. It is having a mindset of loving the Lord with your heart, soul and strength, with everything you have. When your mind is set on Him, you become a target for His blessings. Amen.

Lord, give me the grace to love You with my heart, soul and strength. Help me to live my life to honor You daily in Jesus' name.
Amen.

_____

_____

_____

_____

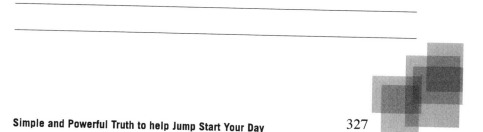

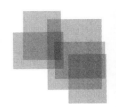

Day 323
Your Grant

*"You have granted me life
and favor, And Your care
has preserved my spirit."*

Job 10:12

You have a grant from the Almighty God, and that grant is the gift of life. This gift is unlimited favor and the preservation of your spirit. In other words, every area of your life is covered by this grant. Do not have a defeated mentality; have an abundant mentality. Start using your grant today. Amen.

*Lord, I thank You for the gift of life, unlimited favor
and for preserving my spirit. Help me to be filled
with faith in Jesus' name.
Amen.*

_____

_____

_____

_____

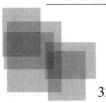

Simple and Powerful Truth to help Jump Start Your Day

Day 324
Speak the Truth

"Therefore, putting away lying,
'Let each one of you speak truth
with his neighbor,' for we are
members of one another."

Ephesians 4:25

The best way to speak the truth is by the way you exemplify the way you live your life. When people see Christ through you, it is much easier for them to listen to You. Christ is love, so speak the truth in love, not in judgment. People respond more to love than they do to criticism. Amen.

Lord, give me the grace to live my life to honor
You so that others can see You through me. Help to
speak the truth in love in Jesus' name.
Amen.

_____

_____

_____

_____

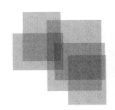

Day 325
Breaking Forth

*"Then your light shall break forth
like the morning, Your healing shall
spring forth speedily, And your
righteousness shall go before you;
The glory of the Lord shall be
your rear guard."*

Isaiah 58:8

You are about to breakout into abundance of everything that is good.
That struggle is coming to an end, and your story will be the next success
story. You will soon be celebrated. Get ready for your victory dance. Amen.

*Lord, I thank You, for You are my peace, joy, hope
and my everything. I will trust in You in Jesus' name.
Amen.*

_____

_____

_____

_____

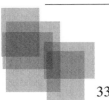

Day 326
Incline Your Heart

" 'Now therefore,' he said,
'put away the foreign gods which
are among you, and incline your
heart to the Lord God of Israel.' "

Joshua 24:23

What and who are you putting before God? Is it money, spouse, a child, business, job, friend or your possessions? All of these have limitations, but God has no limitation. Incline your heart to the Lord. He knows everything about you and what you need. When you put Him first, all other things in your life will come together.

Lord, give me the grace to put you first in my
heart, in my life and to serve You with everything
within me in Jesus' name.
Amen.

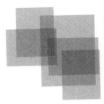

Day 327
Justified and Redeemed

*"For all have sinned and fall short
of the glory of God, being justified
freely by His grace through the
redemption that is in Christ Jesus."*

Romans 3:23-24

We were all sinners, but through Christ Jesus we are justified and redeemed.
When you fall into sin, do not run away from God, run to God.
Receive His forgiveness, justification and redemption. God is not mad at
you when you sin against Him. He is madly in love with you.
Get back up and receive His mercy to do better next time. Amen.

*Lord, thank You for Your justification and
Your redemption. Give me the grace to live my life to
honor You and when I fall short, give me the grace
to run to You in Jesus' name.
Amen.*

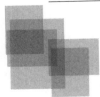

Simple and Powerful Truth to help Jump Start Your Day

Day 328
Complete in Him

"And you are complete in Him..."

Colossians 2:10

You cannot find completion in your spouse, friends, possessions, drugs or any form of addiction. Whatever it is that is missing in your life you can find in Jesus Christ. You are complete in Jesus Christ and in His fullness. Everything about your life is complete in Him; your health, wealth and family are complete in Him. Run to Him and ask Him to help you. Amen.

Lord, give me the grace to fully enjoy
Your complete work of salvation in every area
of my life. I thank You that I am complete
in You in Jesus' name.
Amen.

_____

_____

_____

_____

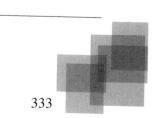

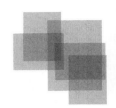

Day 329
Failed Righteousness

*"Also He spoke this parable to
some who trusted in themselves
that they were righteous,
and despised others."*

Luke 18:9

Your righteousness will fail you. You are who you are, because of
Jesus Christ and His grace upon your life. Do not judge or criticize others
who do not believe like you do or acted differently than you do. Love all
and rely on His grace daily to live a life of righteousness. Amen.

*Lord, I thank You for making Your righteousness
to become mine in Jesus' name.
Amen.*

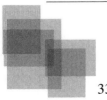

Simple and Powerful Truth to help Jump Start Your Day

Day 330
Guard Your Mouth

"He who guards his mouth
preserves his life,
But he who opens wide his
lips shall have destruction."

Proverbs 13:3

One of the ways to preserves your life and others' lives is to guard your mouth. What you say about yourself and others can create or destroy. Think before you speak even when you are angry. Let the words of your mouth be filled with compassion, grace and encouragement. Amen.

Lord, give me the grace to guard my mouth with
all diligence in Jesus' name.
Amen.

_____

_____

_____

_____

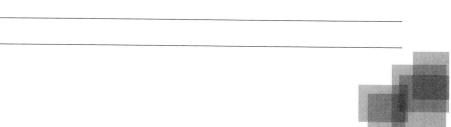

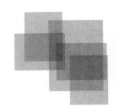

Day 331
Profitable Word

*"For indeed the gospel was
preached to us as well as to them;
but the word which they heard did
not profit them, not being mixed
with faith in those who heard it."*

Hebrews 4:2

I can speak the word of victory, hope, healing and prosperity over your life.
It might not be profitable to you or have maximum impacts in your life,
due to lack of faith. When you hear, read and study the word, let it be
mixed with faith; put actions behind your faith. God will amaze you with
His goodness. Amen.

*Lord, give me the grace to receive Your word into my
life by faith in Jesus' name.
Amen.*

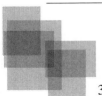

Simple and Powerful Truth to help Jump Start Your Day

Day 332
Prosper by Focus

"Only be strong and very courageous, that you may observe to do according to all the law which Moses My servant commanded you; do not turn from it to the right hand or to the left, that you may prosper wherever you go."

Joshua 1:7

What you focus on expands and eventually dominates your life, and it can become your reality. Prosper by focusing on and declaring the promises of God over your life. Focus on what the word of God says to do about your life and do it diligently. You are on your way to victory. Amen.

Lord, give me the grace to focus on You instead of on my problems or a person in Jesus' name.
Amen.

_____

_____

_____

_____

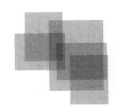

Day 333
Assured

"Most assuredly, I say to you,
he who hears My word and
believes in Him who sent Me has
everlasting life, and shall not come
into judgment, but has passed
from death into life."

John 5:24

When you believe and declare the promises of God over your life and over that situation, you are assured to have things turn around in your favor. You are assured salvation and everything that pertains to life and godliness. Do not speak your fear; speak the word of God over that situation. Amen.

Lord, give me the grace to believe, declare, and live
by Your word in every area of my life in Jesus' name.
Amen.

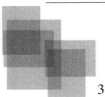

338   **Simple and Powerful Truth to help Jump Start Your Day**

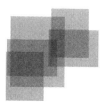

Day 334
Be Fruitful

"By this My Father is glorified,
that you bear much fruit;
so you will be My disciples. "

John 15:8

If you are not growing in every area of your life, you are dying. Give up your excuses and start taking baby steps towards greatness. Start doing your best to start bearing good fruit in your life and in your relationships. Be fruitful! Amen.

Lord, give me the grace to bear good fruit in every
area of my life in Jesus' name.
Amen.

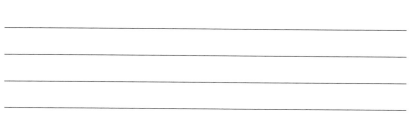

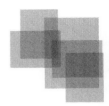

Day 334
Avoid Envy and Strife

"For where envy and self-seeking exist, confusion and every evil thing are there."

James 3:16

Avoid people that create envy and strife. They create confusion and every form of evil you can think of. You do not want that in your life; you are made for more. You can't be everything to everyone. Be wise about with whom you spend your time. Amen.

Lord, give me the grace over any form of envy and strife in my life. Help me to live my life to honor You in Jesus' name.
Amen.

_____

_____

_____

_____

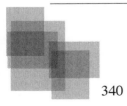

Simple and Powerful Truth to help Jump Start Your Day

Day 336
His Instruction Equals Rest

"Blessed is the man whom You instruct, O Lord, And teach out of Your law, That You may give him rest from the days of adversity, Until the pit is dug for the wicked."

Psalms 94:12-13

God instructs us through His Word. Everything you will ever need for any area of your life can be found in the Word of God. When you follow His instructions you will have rest in the face of difficult situation. Do not worry just follow the Word! Amen.

Lord, give me the grace to follow the instructions
in Your word in Jesus' name.
Amen.

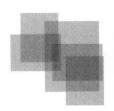

Day 337
Fight the Good Fight

*"Fight the good fight of faith,
lay hold on eternal life, to which
you were also called and have
confessed the good confession in
the presence of many witnesses."*

1 Timothy 6:12

Something is fighting for your attention daily. Who and what you give your attention to will determine your success. Do not give attention to fear, doubt and unbelief. Fight the good fight of faith by paying attention to the word, believing and declaring the word over your life. Amen.

*Lord, give me the grace to fight the good fight
of faith. Let You be the anchor for my soul
in Jesus' name.
Amen.*

_____

_____

_____

_____

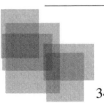

Simple and Powerful Truth to help Jump Start Your Day

Day 338
Results

*"Now no chastening seems to
be joyful for the present, but
painful; nevertheless, afterward
it yields the peaceable fruit of
righteousness to those who have
been trained by it."*

Hebrews 12:11

You are constantly producing results in every area of your life daily.
What kind of results are you producing? It might be painful to discipline
your flesh and be disciplined with what you eat, but the results are
tremendous. They positively affect every area of your life. Start taking
baby steps towards greatness. Amen.

*Lord, give me the grace to overcome neglects in
my life and help me to start taking baby steps to
better my life in Jesus' name.
Amen.*

_____

_____

_____

_____

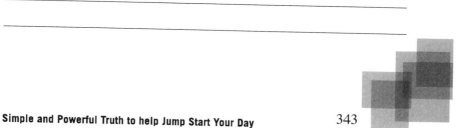

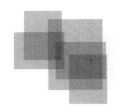

Day 339
Sun and Shield

"For the Lord God is
a sun and shield..."

Psalms 84:11

The Lord is your protector day and night. You do not have to fear anyone or anything. You just need to ask and thank God for His protection from every evil work. He is your sun and shield; trust in Him today. Amen.

Lord, I thank You for You are my sun and shield.
I will trust in You in Jesus' name.
Amen.

_____

_____

_____

_____

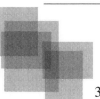

Simple and Powerful Truth to help Jump Start Your Day

Day 340
Grace and Glory

*"The Lord will give
grace and glory..."*

Psalms 84:11

In the midst of that difficult situation, the Lord will give you grace to overcome. He will cause you to come out better off that you were before. He will give you grace and glory. Those who are looking down on you will look up to you; you will be lifted up. Amen.

*Lord, I thank You for giving me grace and glory.
I thank You for lifting me up over every situation
confronting me in Jesus' name.
Amen.*

_____

_____

_____

_____

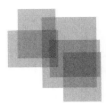

Day 341
Giver of Good Things

"No good thing will He withhold from those who walk uprightly..."

Psalms 84:11

God wants to amaze you with His goodness and He wants to give you good things in every area of your life. Just keep doing your best to live your life to honor Him daily, and His blessings will overflow your life. Peace, joy, health, prosperity and wisdom will be your portion. Amen.

Lord, I receive every good thing You have in store for me. Give me the grace to live my life to honor You daily in Jesus' name.
Amen.

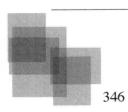

Simple and Powerful Truth to help Jump Start Your Day

Day 342
A New and Living Way

"Therefore, brethren, having boldness to enter the Holiest by the blood of Jesus, by a new and living way which He consecrated for us, through the veil, that is, His flesh."

Hebrews 10:19-20

You do not have to continue to struggle in any area of your life. Jesus died for your salvation and for everything that will make your life better. He came to give you a new and living way. Arise and begin to enjoy your new life. He is your all in all. Amen.

Lord, I thank You for my salvation. Give me the grace to fully enjoy the new and living way you came to give to me in Jesus' name.
Amen.

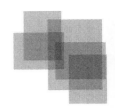

Day 343
I Believe

*"He who believes in Him is not
condemned; but he who does
not believe is condemned already,
because he has not believed
in the name of the only begotten
Son of God."*

John 3:18

I believe in Jesus Christ; I believe He is my healer, my deliverer, my maker, my hope, my peace, my joy, my wisdom, my favor, my protector and my prosperity. I believe Jesus is my everything, because I believe in Him I can never be condemned. Amen.

*Lord, give me the grace to continue to believe in You
no matter what's going on in my life in Jesus' name.
Amen.*

_____

_____

_____

_____

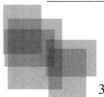

Simple and Powerful Truth to help Jump Start Your Day

Day 344
Die to Grow

"Most assuredly, I say to you, unless a grain of wheat falls into the ground and dies, it remains alone; but if it dies, it produces much grain."

John 12:24

Something has die in you for you to grow. You have to die to a negative mindset to have a positive mindset. You have to die to sin to live a righteous life. For you to grow, something has to die in you. For you to have a great future, you have to be dead to the past. The seed you have been planting in your marriage, health, finances and relationships might be going through a dying period, but if you do not give up, those seeds will produce many fruits. Amen.

Lord, give me the grace to be dead to every limitation in my life so that I can grow and be alive in You in Jesus' name.
Amen.

_____

_____

_____

_____

Day 345
Don't Deceive Yourself

"If we say that we have no sin,
we deceive ourselves,
and the truth is not in us."

1 John 1:8

As humans, we have shortcomings. As believers, we are not perfect beings without sin. Do not put too much pressure on yourself to live a sin-free life. Rely on the grace of God daily to live your life to honor Him. Remember to associate with people who are lifting you up. Amen.

Lord, give me the grace to live my life to honor You
daily in Jesus' name.
Amen.

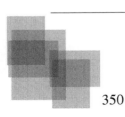

Simple and Powerful Truth to help Jump Start Your Day

Day 346
He Forgives Any Sin

*"If we confess our sins,
He is faithful and just to forgive
us our sins and to cleanse us
from all unrighteousness."*

1 John 1:9

Do not ever feel condemned if you commit the same sin over and over again. Have the mindset to overcome that sin and always go back to God for His forgiveness. Do not indulge yourself in the sin and do not beat yourself up. Ask for His forgiveness and the grace to do better next time. Amen

*Lord, give me grace to always come back to You
when I fall short and the grace to receive Your
forgiveness in Jesus' name.
Amen.*

Day 347
Most Assuredly

"...Most assuredly, I say to you,
whatever you ask the Father in
My name He will give you."

John 16:23

Jesus Christ is guaranteeing your privilege to ask. When you ask for anything in His name, it will be done for you. Ask in faith for the small and the big things. Ask to overcome that addiction, for healing, breakthrough, favor, protection and wisdom. He wants to amaze you with His blessings. Amen.

Lord, I thank You for answered prayers and I give
You praise that I can ask You for anything that
pertains to life and godliness in Jesus' name.
Amen.

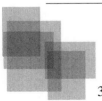

Simple and Powerful Truth to help Jump Start Your Day

Day 348
Full Joy

"Until now you have asked nothing in My name. Ask, and you will receive, that your joy may be full."

John 16:24

If you do not ask, you will not receive. Ask in faith for your breakthrough, deliverance, healing and abundance. Ask in faith for grace to live a life of righteousness, for your child, marriage, job, business, city, nation and the world. God takes pleasure in blessing you so that your joy may be made full. Amen.

Lord, give me the grace to ask in faith for every area of my life. I thank You for Your full joy in my life in Jesus' name.
Amen.

_____

_____

_____

_____

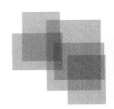

Day 349
Be Consistent

"Now when Daniel knew that the writing was signed, he went home. And in his upper room, with his windows open toward Jerusalem, he knelt down on his knees three times that day, and prayed and gave thanks before his God, as was his custom since early days."

Daniel 6:10

What you do consistently on a daily basis can make or break you. Is what you do daily in every area of your life increasing or decreasing you? Do the positive and what works consistently in your life. Pray and give thanks, read and study the Bible on daily basis. Start taking baby steps daily towards a great life.

Lord, give me the grace to do what works according to Your word consistently in my life daily in Jesus' name.
Amen.

_____

_____

_____

_____

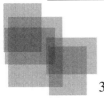

Simple and Powerful Truth to help Jump Start Your Day

Day 350
Redeemer and Profit Maker

"Thus says the Lord,
your Redeemer, The Holy One of
Israel: 'I am the Lord your God,
Who teaches you to profit,
Who leads you by the way
you should go.'"

Isaiah 48:17

God did not only redeem you from the curse of sin and death; He wants you to prosper and have more than enough in every area of your life. He wants to teach you how to have profitable endeavors. It is His delight to prosper you. Gladly receive His blessings into your life today. Amen.

Lord, teach me to profit in every area of my life.
I receive Your blessings into my life in Jesus'
name. Amen.

_____

_____

_____

_____

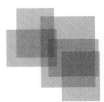

Day 351
A Season and a Purpose

*"To everything there is a
season, A time for every
purpose under heaven."*

Ecclesiastes 3:1

Make the most of everything. Do not waste your disappointments; learn
from them. Enjoy your life to the fullest. Do not meddle with minor things
and minor people. Focus on the good, enjoy the moment and enjoy the
season. Amen.

*Lord, give me the grace to make the most of every
season in my life in Jesus' name.
Amen,*

_____

_____

_____

_____

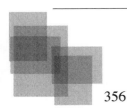

Simple and Powerful Truth to help Jump Start Your Day

Day 352
Increasing in Fruitfulness

*"...that you may walk worthy
of the Lord, fully pleasing Him,
being fruitful in every good
work and increasing in the
knowledge of God..."*

Colossians 1:10

Your life never remains stagnant; you are either moving forward or backward, increasing or decreasing. Do what is causing you to increase in fruitfulness in every aspect of your life. Stop any form of excuses and begin to increase in fruitfulness. Amen.

*Lord, give me the grace to increase in fruitfulness
in every area of my life in Jesus' name.
Amen.*

_____

_____

_____

_____

Day 353
A New Song

"He has put a new song in my mouth— Praise to our God; many will see it and fear, and will trust in the Lord."

Psalms 40:3

God wants to put a new song of victory in your mouth. He wants to amaze you with His goodness. Get ready for a shout of praise, get ready for a song of victory and get ready for a dance of breakthrough. You are the next success story. Amen.

Lord, I thank You for filling my mouth with new songs of victory. I praise you O Lord in Jesus' name. Amen.

_____

_____

_____

_____

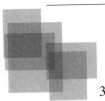

Simple and Powerful Truth to help Jump Start Your Day

Day 354
You Are Coming Out

"He also brought me up out of a horrible pit, Out of the miry clay, and set my feet upon a rock, And established my steps."

Psalms 40:2

You are coming out of that situation. Every stronghold has been broken. You are being lifted up, and every chain of addiction is destroyed in your life. You are coming out into joy, peace, freedom, wisdom and abundance. Amen.

Lord, I thank You for causing me to come into Your victory and breakthroughs in Jesus' name. Amen.

_____

_____

_____

_____

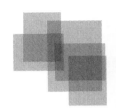

Day 355
He Answers

"I waited patiently for the Lord;
And He inclined to me,
and heard my cry."

Psalms 40:1

No matter what is confronting you, God already provided a solution to it.
Do not get frustrated; instead give thanks to God for answering your
prayers. Be patient knowing that God has inclined His ears to your prayers.
Do not worry about your timing; He knows the best and He knows what
you need and the right time to get it to you. It is well with you. Amen.

Lord, I thank You for answered prayers. Give me the
grace to be patient with Your timing in Jesus' name.
Amen.

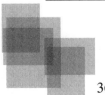

Simple and Powerful Truth to help Jump Start Your Day

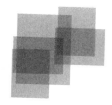

Day 356
Be Still

"Be still, and know that I am God; I will be exalted among the nations, I will be exalted in the earth!"

Psalms 46:10

Maybe you have done all that you know to do about that situation and gotten little or no result. My friend, don't worry; be still, because God is about to exalt you and do the impossible in your life. Keep doing your best and don't try to figure everything out. Just be still and let God be Lord over that situation. Amen.

Lord, I choose to trust in You. Give me the grace to be still and to totally depend on You in Jesus' name. Amen.

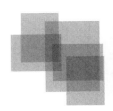

Day 357
It's Not About You

"Now when they saw the boldness
of Peter and John, and perceived
that they were uneducated and
untrained men, they marveled.
And they realized that they had
been with Jesus."

Acts 4:13

God can do the incredible through you regardless of your talents, skills and abilities. If you are faithful, God will use you in a great and mighty way. Do not worry about what you do not have or who you do not know. You have God; He knows who and what you need and He knows how to get them to you. Amen.

Lord, I surrender to You. Use me for the glory of
Your name in Jesus' name.
Amen.

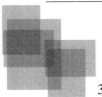

Simple and Powerful Truth to help Jump Start Your Day

Day 358
New You

*"Therefore, if anyone is in Christ,
he is a new creation; old things
have passed away; behold,
all things have become new."*

2 Corinthians 5:17

Jesus came to give you a new life. When you commit your life to Him, He will give you a new you. Things might not change overnight, but something changed on the inside of you. He is working in you and perfecting you. Amen.

*Lord, I thank You for the new life You came to give
me. Give me the grace to fully live this new life
in Jesus' name.
Amen.*

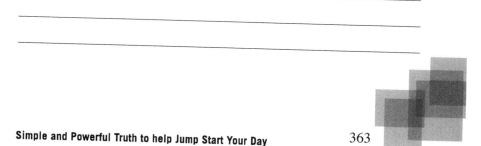

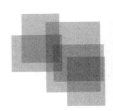

Day 359
Hunger for Wisdom

"Get wisdom! Get understanding!
Do not forget, nor turn away from
the words of my mouth."

Proverbs 4:5

Wisdom gives you a shortcut to success in life. The word of God is full of wisdom for every area of your life. When faced with a situation, instead of worrying, get wisdom. Read, research, study and intentionally internalize the wisdom of God in your life. Amen.

Lord, give me the grace to hunger and thirst after
wisdom and help me to apply Your wisdom into my
life in Jesus' name.
Amen.

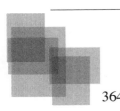

Simple and Powerful Truth to help Jump Start Your Day

Day 360
Hunger for Righteousness

*"Blessed are those who hunger
and thirst for righteousness,
For they shall be filled."*

Matthew 5:6

Living a righteous life produces tremendous benefits in every aspect of your life. Righteousness does not mean perfection; it means having a right standing with God. It is having a mind set to live your life to honor God. Develop an intense hunger for righteousness. When you fall, receive His forgiveness and continue in your walk of holiness.

*Lord, give me the grace to be hunger and thirsty
after righteousness in Jesus' name.
Amen.*

Day 361
Write Down the Vision

"Write the vision
And make it plain on tablets,
That he may run who reads it."

Habakkuk 2:2

Your eyes give you vision to see physical things. Having a vision for your life gives you something to look forward to, empowers you, encourages you and allows you to have a sense of direction. Write the vision down for your life and make it clear to follow. Amen.

Lord, give me the wisdom to write the vision down
for my life and give me the grace to live my vision
in Jesus' name.
Amen.

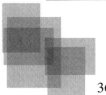

Simple and Powerful Truth to help Jump Start Your Day

Day 362
Small Becoming Big

"Though your beginning was small, Yet your latter end would increase abundantly."

Job 8:7

God can use you wherever you are with whatever you have. Do not look down on yourself and belittle the little that you have. Be faithful and start taking baby steps; before you know it the small will become big. Your best is yet to come. Amen.

Lord, give me the grace to recognize what I have in my hand and the grace to be faithful with it in Jesus' name.
Amen.

_____

_____

_____

_____

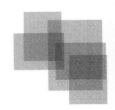

Day 363
Never Give Up

"Blessed is the man who endures
temptation; for when he has been
approved, he will receive the crown
of life which the Lord has promised
to those who love Him."

James 1:12

Never give up no matter how many times you have tried and failed.
Get back up, endure and keep moving forward. Do not allow a habitual
temptation to make you feel condemned. Ask God for help to overcome
and keep on enduring. Never give up! Amen.

Lord, give me the grace to endure temptations and
help me to live my life to honor You in Jesus' name.
Amen.

_____

_____

_____

_____

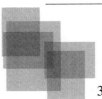

Simple and Powerful Truth to help Jump Start Your Day

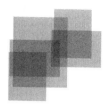

Day 364
He Is With You!

*"For the Lord your God is He
who goes with you, to fight for
you against your enemies, to save
you."*

Deuteronomy 20:4

In the midst of that difficulty, picture the Lord your God beside you and going before you, making crooked way straight and fighting your enemies. He is fighting for you against the enemy of fear, depression, sickness, lack, confusion and loneliness, to save you. He is with you. Trust in Him today to fight your battles for you. Amen.

*Lord, I thank You for being with me and for
fighting my battles for me. Give me grace to focus
on You, instead of the situation confronting me
in Jesus name.
Amen.*

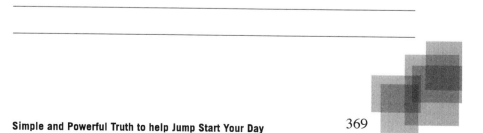

Day 365
Ask for Help

"Let us therefore come boldly to the throne of grace, that we may obtain mercy and find grace to help in time of need."

Hebrews 4:16

When the going gets tough, the tough ask for help. Asking for help is not a sign of weakness; it is a sign of humility and strength. God is willing to help you and He can also use others to help you. You do not have to fight the addiction, sickness, relationship problems and spiritual, physical, mental and emotional problems on your own. Ask for help with confidence. Amen.

Lord, give me the grace to ask for help when needed.
I rely on and I trust in You in Jesus' name.
Amen.

Simple and Powerful Truth to help Jump Start Your Day

I Will Not Fail You or Forsake You

"There shall not any man be able to stand before thee all the days of thy life: as I was with Moses, so I will be with you: I will not fail (nosedive, bomb, flop, miscarry, crash, stop, die, collapse and disappoint) you, nor forsake (abandon, desert, leave, disown, quit, ditch, reject, renounce, relinquish and sacrifice) you."

Joshua 1:5 KJV

No matter what is going on in your life, no matter how far or how low you've gone, your Heavenly Father promise to not fail you or forsake you and He wants you to enjoy every area of your life to the fullest. Don't stop. Re-read, re-meditate and re-declare this devotional again. I'm excited about the testimonies of God's goodness in every aspect of your life. Amen.

_____

_____

_____

_____

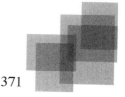

About the Author

Gbenga Asedeko is a *dynamic and enthusiastic* motivational speaker, *celebrated* author, trainer, coach and consultant. *He* was born and raised in Nigeria, West Africa *were* Growing up was very challenging. *Gbenga* taught himself to read and write effectively *and* his resolve *to succeed* has inspired many in both Nigeria and the United States. He earned a bachelor's degree in accounting and an MBA from the University of Texas at El Paso (UTEP). He is a Distinguished Toastmaster, the highest honor by Toastmasters International in communication and leadership.

While attending UTEP he served as the student body president for two years. He was the General Manager of El Paso Pulmonary Association (EPPA), the largest subspecialty pulmonary group in the southwest region of United States. Before joining EPPA he worked with the Centers for Entrepreneurial Development Advancement and Research Services as a business specialist. His background includes a wide range of business development, project management, sales, accounting, and effective management of human resources.

Gbenga has made a *lasting* difference in the lives of students, athletes, Olympians, youths, and professionals. *His* client *list includes* El Paso Department of Public Health, The University of Texas at El Paso, El Paso Mortgage Bankers Association, Golden Real Estate Company, Tri State Mortgage Company, Sodexho Food Services and Spira Shoes. Gbenga believes that everything in our lives rises and falls on our relationships with God and that the more time we invest in our relationship with God the better our lives will get. His unique interactive speaking style engages his audience by getting them to participate and always being relevant has made Gbenga a much sought-after speaker.

He lives in El Paso, Texas, with his wife, Marisela, and their sons, Jordan G.Q. and Jaden G.Q.

www.GbengaAsedeko.com

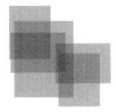

Made in the USA
Charleston, SC
13 March 2015